Happy Birthday

from

Carolyn Haywood

Books by Carolyn Haywood

Summer Fun 1986

Merry Christmas from Eddie 1986

How the Reindeer Saved Santa 1986

Happy Birthday from Carolyn Haywood 1984

Santa Claus Forever! 1983

Halloween Treats 1981

The King's Monster 1980

Eddie's Menagerie 1978

Betsy's Play School 1977

A Valentine Fantasy 1976

Eddie's Valuable Property 1975

''C'' Is for Cupcake 1974

Away Went the Balloons 1973

A Christmas Fantasy 1972

Eddie's Happenings 1971

Merry Christmas from Betsy 1970

Taffy and Melissa Molasses 1969

Ever-Ready Eddie 1968

Betsy and Mr. Kilpatrick 1967

Eddie the Dog Holder 1966

Robert Rows the River 1965

Eddie's Green Thumb 1964

Here Comes the Bus! 1963

Snowbound with Betsy 1962

Happy Birthday
from
Carolyn Haywood

by CAROLYN HAYWOOD
pictures by WENDY WATSON

Troll Associates

A TROLL BOOK, published by Troll Associates,
Mahwah, NJ 07430

Published by arrangement with William Morrow and Company,
Inc. For information address William Morrow and Company,
Inc., 105 Madison Avenue, New York, New York 10016.

First Troll Printing, 1987

Printed in the United States of America

10 9 8 7 6 5 4 3 2 1

ISBN 0-8167-1040-6

To Lucy Nalle
and her big sister Ellen,
with love.

Contents

Happy Birthday
from
Carolyn Haywood

One

Betsy's Easter Birthday

Betsy would soon be eight years old. The date fell on the Saturday before Easter. Betsy was surprised when her mother told her that her birthday would be the Saturday before Easter. Betsy said, "I don't remember that my birthday ever was at Easter time before."

"That is because the date for Easter is not always the same," her mother said. "It isn't always on the same date, or even in the same month.

Sometimes it's in April and sometimes in March. But it so happens this year that it is in April. And your birthday is on April seventh, the day before Easter."

"I think that's nice," said Betsy. "We can have an Easter egg hunt in the yard for the kids."

"Of course," her mother agreed. "I'll dye the eggs, and we'll hide them in the yard."

"Oh, that will be fun, and a different birthday party, not just silly games," said Betsy.

"Yes, I think your guests will enjoy it," said her mother. "Now, Betsy, you must tell me who you wish to invite to your birthday party. I'll write down their names on this pad."

"Begin with Ellen," said Betsy.

"Of course," said her mother. "And then, I suppose, Billy Porter."

"No!" Betsy cried out.

Betsy's mother looked at her in surprise. "Why, Betsy," she said. "Not Billy Porter? You play to-gether so much."

"No boys!" said Betsy. "I'm not going to have any boys at my parties ever! Boys spoil parties.

They wrestle and throw things. I don't know why boys have to throw things. At the last birthday party I went to, they even threw pieces of birthday cake at each other. I'm not having any boys at my party. Just girls."

"Very well," said Betsy's mother. "No boys!"

"That's right," said Betsy. And she began to call out the names of eight girls, while her mother wrote them down.

"Don't you want more than eight?" her mother asked.

"No," said Betsy. "I've decided I'm always going to have just the number as my age. I'm going to be eight years old, and I'm having eight girl friends. Next year I'll have nine."

Betsy's mother laughed. "When you're twenty-one, we won't be able to get them around the table! In fact, we don't have twenty-one chairs in the house."

Betsy laughed. "Oh, you'll find a way, Mom. You always find a way. Or Daddy will."

"I'll leave it up to Daddy when the time comes." Her mother laughed.

The following day eight invitations were sent out to the eight girls. They all replied that they would be delighted to come to the party.

The day before the party, when Betsy came home from school, her mother brought out eight dozen eggs.

"Oh!" said Betsy. "Now you're going to dye the eggs."

"Yes," her mother replied. "And I have gold trimming to fasten on the colored eggs."

Betsy was excited. "Oh, I can't wait to see them!" she said. "This birthday party is going to be super! There never was a birthday party like this party."

Betsy spent the evening decorating the colored Easter eggs. There were blue eggs, green eggs, purple eggs—all colors. And when they were trimmed with gold, Betsy thought they were very beautiful. Now they were ready to hide under bushes and behind trees in the yard. This would be done before Betsy's friends arrived.

By two o'clock on Saturday Betsy was dressed in her birthday dress and waiting for her guests.

Then the telephone rang. Betsy picked up the receiver and said, "Hello. This is Betsy."

"I'm sorry, Betsy," said her friend Ellen's voice, "but I can't come to the party. I have to go with my mother to see my grandfather. He isn't feeling well."

"Oh, that's too bad!" said Betsy. "We're going to have a lot of fun hunting for Easter eggs. We'll miss you!"

A few minutes later the telephone rang again. Betsy picked it up. It was Mary Lou. She sounded all choked up. "My mother won't let me go out because I have a cold. I'm so sorry I'm going to miss your party." Mary Lou sounded as though she was crying.

"Oh, I'm sorry," said Betsy, feeling disappointed that another friend had dropped out of the party.

When three o'clock arrived and no one had appeared, Betsy said to her mother, "Maybe nobody's coming to my party."

"The clock has just struck three," said her mother. "Don't start fretting."

Betsy tried to be patient. But by ten after three, no one had arrived. "I think the others forgot about my party!" said Betsy.

Then Rosemary telephoned. "Oh, Betsy," she said. "I started out for your party but I fell and hurt my leg. I'm sorry I can't come."

"That's too bad," said Betsy. "I hope you didn't hurt it badly." Then Betsy said to her mother, "I guess everybody fell down! I don't think I'm going to have any party after all. And I'll have to gather up all those eggs."

Betsy's father, who had just come in, said, "Of course you're going to have a party."

Betsy sobbed. "Well, you have to have friends for a party," she said, "and my friends have disappointed me." By now Betsy was crying in earnest.

"Betsy, dear, dry your tears," said her father. "And trust your daddy. He's the miracle man around here!"

Her father went out, and from the front window Betsy watched him get into his station wagon and drive away. Betsy stood for a long time by the window, watching for her father's return.

As it struck three-thirty, the telephone rang. Betsy rushed to answer it. "Is that you, Betty Jane?" she asked. "What's the matter?"

Betty Jane, sounding very excited, said, "Oh, Betsy! My mother can't get the car started. She thinks it's the battery."

"Betty Jane," Betsy cried, "You were to bring Susie and Nancy and Rosamond and Margery!"

"I know," said Betty Jane. "Can't your mother come for us?"

"No!" Betsy replied. "Daddy took the car."

"Oh, Betsy!" Betty Jane wailed. "We won't be able to come to your party. I wish Mom could get the car started."

"Well, look," said Betsy, "if she can get the car started, come, even if you don't get here until late. I have this beautiful birthday cake, and I can't bear to have my party washed out."

Betsy returned to the window, and shortly before four o'clock, she saw her father return. She saw her father step out of the car, and then to her great surprise she saw her friend Billy Porter, wearing his Little League uniform, step out, followed by Kenny Roberts. Now the twins, Richard and Henry, were getting out, both in their uniforms. Betsy watched in amazement, for the station wagon seemed to be full of boys.

Now her father opened the front door, and Billy and Kenny came in. "Hi, Betsy!" said Billy. "Happy birthday!"

"Yes," said Kenny. "Happy birthday!"

Then the two boys began talking at the same time. "You know, Betsy," said Billy, "we're in the Little League."

"You betcha!" said Kenny. "And we waited since twelve o'clock for the team we were to play."

"That's right," said Billy, "and they never showed up."

Now the twins had come in, and Richard said, "But your dad came along."

"That's right," said Henry. "And your dad yelled, 'Hey, fellows! Do you want to go to a party?'"

By now Betsy was surrounded by the whole Little League team from her class in school—nine boys with bats, balls and gloves. "And your dad said," shouted Richard, "that there would be ice cream and a birthday cake!"

"He sure did," said Henry. "And I can see the cake on the table now. Does it look good!"

Betsy felt much better now that somebody had come to her party. She even felt glad to have nine boys. Betsy was so excited at having these sudden guests that she didn't think of sending her father for the girls. She lifted her voice above their chatter and said, "First we're going to hunt for Easter eggs in the yard!"

Betsy led the way and the boys, eager to find the Easter eggs, rushed out into the yard. Soon their voices could be heard. "I found one!" "Oh boy! They're neat!" "I've got a purple one." "I guess a purple hen laid it!"

Then came Billy's voice, "Hey! I haven't found any eggs. You fellows have grabbed all of them."

Betsy called back, "Look some more, Billy. Look in the rock garden."

Billy went off to the rock garden. In a few minutes he called out, "Hey, guys, I've found gold! There's gold here."

Richard called back, "Go on, Bill! It's the gold trimming on the egg." Billy picked up an egg and looked at it. He said, "Oh, drat. I thought I had found my fortune."

The egg hunt came to an end now, for Betsy's mother called the boys in for the party food. Soon they were gathered around the table where ten plates of ice cream were waiting for them. Betsy blew out the candles on her cake and cut each boy a large slice.

There was a bright paper tube beside each plate, and everyone knew what was inside, for they had been to parties before. The boys picked them up and each one was opened with a bang. Then each boy put a funny hat on his head, and the whole room was full of laughter as the boys looked at each other. The hats, with their Little League uniforms, made them look so funny. They laughed and laughed, pointing to each other.

When the party was over, the boys gathered up their bats, balls and gloves, and as they left they all said, "Thanks for the party!"

When Billy said good-bye, he said, "Sorry I

don't have a birthday present for you, Betsy! Of course, I could give you my bat, but I guess you wouldn't have much use for a baseball bat."

"Well, it was nice of you to think of it, Billy," said Betsy. Then she stood by the window again and watched her father drive off with the nine boys. Just as the license plate disappeared around the corner, Betty Jane's mother drove up.

"Oh, Mom," Betsy cried out, "here's Betty Jane's mother with the girls. Oh, what will we do? The boys ate all of the birthday cake! There is not a crumb left."

"Go let them in," said her mother, "and don't worry. I have a beautiful apple pie. I'll just put the birthday candles on it and you will have a birthday pie."

"Oh, that's great, Mom!" said Betsy as she opened the door. "You always find a way out. I never had a birthday pie before, and I think it is a wonderful idea."

As the girls came in, Betsy was pleased to see that each girl had a birthday present in her hand. At last, she was going to have some birthday presents on her eighth birthday. Everyone seemed to enjoy the birthday pie with ice cream.

As the girls left, Betty Jane said, "That was real clever of you, Betsy, to have a birthday pie."

"I thought so, too," said Betsy, as she winked at her mother.

Two

The Forgotten Birthday Cake

Jonathan Mason had been looking forward to his sixth birthday. It would be his first birthday in his new home, for he and his mother and father had just moved to a farmhouse in the country. Jonathan had started the first grade.

One day he said to his mother, "Mommy, do you think Miss Adams would let me have my birthday party at school?"

"I don't know, Jon," his mother replied. "Why don't you ask her?"

"I could take my birthday cake to school on the bus," said Jonathan.

"I suppose you could," said his mother.

"What about ice cream?" Jonathan asked.

"Ice cream is delivered to the school every day, for the lunchroom," said his mother. "I'll buy enough ice cream for the first grade."

"Oh, goody!" said Jonathan. "I'll ask Miss Adams if we can have the party."

The next morning, when Jonathan went into his classroom, he went up to Miss Adams. "Good morning, Miss Adams," he said. "Can I whisper something to you?"

"What is it?" Miss Adams asked, leaning over.

"My mommy says she will buy the ice cream if I can have my birthday party here in school," said Jonathan. "I want to invite all the children in the first grade. I'm glad everybody in my room is in the first grade. It's cozy, isn't it?"

"Yes," said Miss Adams. "In this school each grade is in one classroom. It's different, but out here in the country we like it. I think a party would be lovely! When is your birthday?"

"Next Friday," replied Jonathan. "I'll bring a birthday cake, too."

"It sounds wonderful!" said Miss Adams.

"You won't tell, will you?" said Jonathan.

"No indeed," replied his teacher.

"It will be a surprise party," said Jonathan.

Miss Adams laughed, and said, "Usually the person having the birthday is the one who is surprised."

Jonathan laughed, too. Then he said, "Yes, but this time everybody is going to be surprised except me."

Melissa heard what Jonathan said, and called out, "What's the surprise?"

"It's a secret," said Miss Adams.

"When will we know?" asked Melissa.

"Next Friday," said Jonathan.

When Jonathan reached home that afternoon, he rushed into the house and called out, "Mommy! Miss Adams says I can have a birthday party!"

"That's good news!" said his mother. "What kind of birthday cake shall I make?"

"A big one!" Jonathan replied.

"Of course!" his mother said.

"Make that one that tastes like butter," said Jonathan. "And a lot of thick white icing. And red candles."

"Red candles are for Christmas," said his mother.

"I like red," said Jonathan.

"Very well," said his mother. "I'll get red candles. Instead of everyone singing 'Happy Birthday,' they can all sing 'Jolly Old Saint Nicholas.'"

Jonathan laughed and hung his jacket in the hall closet.

The day before Jonathan's birthday, his mother made the cake. When he came home, it was on the kitchen table. It was covered all over with creamy white icing, and it looked beautiful. It was the biggest birthday cake Jonathan had ever seen.

"I'm going to put the cake in this hatbox," said his mother, holding up a round hatbox. "You'll have to carry it carefully, Jon."

"I'll carry it carefully, all right," said Jonathan. "I don't want anything to happen to my birthday cake."

The following morning Jonathan's cake was packed away in the hatbox. His mother packed it very carefully. It was covered with wax paper, and rolls of wax paper kept the sides of the cake from rubbing against the box. The lid was tied down with a strong cord. "I'll carry it to the bus for you, Jon," said his mother.

"Oh no! Mommy, I can carry it," said Jonathan. "I want to carry it myself."

"But you have your lunch box to carry and your books," said his mother.

"I'll carry my books on my back," said Jonathan. "And I have two hands!"

"You can't carry the cake box by the string," said his mother. "You'll need both hands."

"Well, I can do it!" said Jonathan, as he put on his jacket. "I'll show you." When Jonathan picked up the box, his arms were full.

"Now how are you going to carry your lunch box?" his mother asked.

"On top," said Jonathan.

"All right," said his mother, "but if you drop the cake, you'll have to have your party with a broken birthday cake."

"I won't drop it," said Jonathan, as he went out the door. "I'll walk slowly."

Jonathan couldn't see where he was walking very well. Once he tripped over a stone in the road, but he caught himself and didn't drop anything. By the time he reached the mailboxes by the main road, the birthday cake seemed heavier than it had when he started out. It was too heavy to hold until the bus arrived.

Jonathan looked around for a place to rest the box. He didn't want to put it on the ground. A bug might get into it. He decided that the best place would be right on top of the mailboxes. Mr. Tattersall, who was farming the Masons' land, had his mailbox right beside Jonathan's. It leaned toward it in a friendly kind of way. Together the two mailboxes made a big enough shelf to hold the birthday cake. Jonathan put it down very carefully. Then he felt it to see if it was steady. He didn't want anything to happen to that cake.

Jonathan stood waiting for the bus with his lunch box in his hand. He kicked the fallen leaves that lay beside the road. Then he looked up at the trees. Their black branches were almost bare against the blue sky. He sniffed the air. For weeks it had been filled with the odor of burning leaves. He looked down at the leaves. He saw red leaves, pink leaves, purple leaves, brown leaves, and leaves every color of yellow, from pale lemon to deep gold. Jonathan began to pick up the ones he thought were the prettiest. As he picked them up, he walked up the road. Here he found a cherry-colored one, there an orange one. Soon he had a large bunch of beautiful leaves. He looked at them carefully and decided to take them to school. Perhaps Miss Adams would like to stick them on the bulletin board.

Jonathan was so busy selecting leaves that he forgot to think about the bus. He had walked quite a way from his own mailbox. Suddenly, as if by magic, the school bus stopped beside him.

When the door opened Mr. Riley, the bus driver called, out, "Hi, Jonny! Were you walking to meet me this morning?"

Jonathan stepped into the bus. "Hi, Rus!" he said. Then he held up the bunch of brightly colored leaves. "Look! Aren't they pretty?"

"Sure are!" said Rus as he closed the door.

Mr. Riley stepped on the gas, and the school bus bounced off. Jonathan sat down without thinking of his birthday cake. He didn't think of it until Melissa said, "Jonny, it's Friday! You said you would tell me your secret on Friday. What's the secret?"

Jonathan jumped up as though he had suddenly sat on a bumblebee. "Oh, Rus!" he cried out, as he rushed up the aisle of the bus. "Rus! I have to go back! I left my birthday cake on the mailbox."

"We can't go back now," said Mr. Riley. "If I go back now, the whole busload will be late for school."

"But it's for my birthday party," said Jonathan.

"I'll go back and get it after I get this crowd to school," said Mr. Riley.

"Where is the birthday party going to be?" asked Melissa.

"At school," replied Jonathan.

"For everybody?" exclaimed Melissa.

"For everybody in our room," said Jonathan.

"You mean with ice cream?" said Melissa.

"Yepper!" replied Jonathan. He was still leaning beside Mr. Riley. "You won't forget to go back and get my birthday cake, will you, Rus?" he said.

"I won't forget," replied Mr. Riley.

"It's on top of the mailboxes," said Jonathan. "It's in one of my mommy's hatboxes."

"Okay!" said Rus.

"You'll have to carry it carefully," said Jonathan, "so it doesn't break."

"Okay, okay!" said Rus. "Sit down and stop pestering me."

By the time the bus reached the school, everyone knew that Jonathan was having a birthday party. Everyone also knew that he had left his birthday cake sitting on top of the mailboxes at the end of the lane. As they got off the bus, the whole first grade reminded Mr. Riley to go back and get the birthday cake.

"I'll get it!" he replied.

While Mr. Riley was driving the school bus back over the country roads, the mailman was driving from mailbox to mailbox. Sometimes the mailman found letters inside the mailbox waiting for him. These he picked up and took with him to the post office. Sometimes there were even packages waiting for him.

The mailman's name was Joe Davis, and he tried very hard to help everybody. He knew that it was hard at times for people who lived out in the country to get to the post office in town.

Not long after the school bus had picked up Jonathan, the mailman stopped to leave some letters for Jonathan's father in the Masons' mailbox. When he stopped his van, he was surprised to find a large round hatbox sitting on top of the mailboxes. Mr. Davis looked at it carefully, turning the box all around. On one side he saw Jonathan's mother's name—Mrs. David Mason. He pushed his hat back and scratched his head. He was puzzled. He wondered what he was supposed to do with this hatbox.

After a few moments, he decided to take it with him. He guessed that Mrs. Mason wanted the hat to go back to the store. He picked it up and placed it on the front seat of his van.

Mr. Davis drove from mailbox to mailbox

along the country roads. He passed fields where the corn had been cut down. He passed apple orchards and called out to the farmers who were gathering the last of the apples. "Morning, Will!" "Morning, Tom!" He knew everybody and everybody knew him.

When Mr. Davis stopped to leave the mail at Mrs. Trimbull's, she was standing beside the mailbox with a letter in her hand. "Morning, Mrs. Trimbull!" said the mailman, as he pulled up beside her. "Think I've got a letter for you this morning."

"Well, I've got one for you," said Mrs. Trimbull. "It's a letter to my grandson. He's in the army now."

"He'll be glad to get that," said Mr. Davis, taking the letter from her. He looked through the letters in his pouch, and muttered, "Now I was sure I had a letter for you. Where did that letter get to?"

Mr. Davis looked on the seat of the van. Then he moved the hatbox and there, behind it, was a bundle of letters. "Ah! There's your letter! Right on top of this bundle. Couldn't see it for this hat-box."

Mr. Davis handed the letter to Mrs. Trimbull, and said, "People do funny things 'round here! Those new people just moved here from a big city. Mason's the name. Well, she left this hatbox sitting right on top of the mailboxes. I guess she thought I'd drop it off at the shop. I brought it along."

"Well, that's good of you, Joe," said Mrs. Trimbull, looking up the road. She looked puzzled, then she said, "Now why do you suppose Rus Riley is driving his school bus back this way? He went past here with the children over a half-hour ago."

The mailman looked up the road. Sure enough! Rus Riley was driving toward them. As he neared the mailman's car, Mr. Riley slowed down. He shifted gears, but he didn't quite stop. As he went by, he called out the window, "I have to go back for a birthday cake. First grader forgot his birth-day cake."

Mr. Davis and Mrs. Trimbull both laughed. "I

don't know what we'd do without Rus and you, Joe," said Mrs. Trimbull. The mailman and Mrs. Trimbull watched the school bus until it disappeared.

When the school bus arrived at the Masons' mailbox, the hatbox, of couse, was gone. "Now what!" Mr. Riley said aloud. Just as Mr. Davis had done, Mr. Riley pushed his hat back and scratched his head. Then he turned the bus into the lane and drove it up to the Masons' house.

Mr. Riley got out of the bus and rang the front doorbell. When Jonathan's mother opened the door, she was surprised to see him and the big yellow school bus. "Why, Mr. Riley!" she exclaimed. "What's the matter?"

"It's that birthday cake!" said Mr. Riley. "Jonny forgot it."

"But he took it with him," said Mrs. Mason.

"Yes, I know, but he left it on top of the mailboxes," said Mr. Riley. "I came back for it, but it's gone."

"Oh, how awful!" said Mrs. Mason. "Who do you suppose took it?"

"I don't know," said Mr. Riley. "Could have been Joe when he left the mail, but I spoke to him on my way out. He didn't say anything to me."

"I'll telephone the post office," said Mrs. Mason. "Maybe he's there."

Mrs. Mason called the post office while Mr. Riley waited in the hall. When she heard a voice on the other end of the telephone, she said, "Has Joe Davis come in?"

"No, ma'am!" was the reply. "Joe won't be in until around three o'clock."

"Thank you," said Jonathan's mother, and she hung up the telephone. She came back to Mr. Riley. "Joe Davis won't be back at the post office until three o'clock. I can't bake another cake, and I can't go into town to buy one, because my husband has our car."

"Wish there was something I could do about it," said Mr. Riley. "I could take you in town, but I couldn't bring you back, so that wouldn't do any good."

Suddenly an idea came to Mrs. Mason. "Oh, Mr. Riley!" she said. "Do you suppose you could buy a birthday cake for me at the bakery in town? Could you take it to school?"

"I don't see why not!" said Mr. Riley.

"Oh, Mr. Riley! That's wonderful!" said Mrs. Mason. "I can't bear to have the children disappointed."

Mrs. Mason gave Mr. Riley the money to pay for the birthday cake. He put it in his pocket and said, "Don't worry about it. I'll get a birthday cake."

Mr. Riley got into the bus and drove off. He drove right to the bakery shop, and he was happy to see that there was a lovely birthday cake.

While the bake shop assistant was packing the cake into a box, Mr. Riley told her about Jonathan leaving his birthday cake on top of the mailbox. They both laughed.

Mr. Riley was soon on his way back to the school.

In the meantime, Mr. Davis was driving over the country roads, leaving the mail in the mailboxes.

After some time, he picked up the hatbox to see

if any more letters had got under the box. When he picked it up, he thought to himself, This is a very heavy hat. He began to wonder whether it was a hat after all.

Mr. Davis decided to look inside the box. He untied the string. Then he lifted the lid. He looked down into a lot of wax paper, and there he saw the birthday cake.

Mr. Davis was very surprised. "A birthday cake!" he said to himself. "Imagine leaving a birthday cake on top of a mailbox!"

Suddenly Mr. Davis remembered that Rus Riley had called out something to him about a birthday cake. He thought a minute. Then he recalled what the bus driver had said. "A first grader forgot his birthday cake."

"Oh, gosh!" Mr. Davis said aloud. "I have to take the birthday cake to the first grade!"

Meanwhile, the school bus flew along the main road to town.

When Mr. Riley reached the school, he opened a side door that led into a long hall. As he entered the hall, he saw a door open on the opposite side of the school. A man stepped into the other end of the hall. As the man came toward Mr. Riley, the bus driver saw that he was also carrying a box. As he came nearer, Mr. Riley saw that the man was Joe Davis, the mailman.

When the mailman recognized his friend Rus Riley, he called out, "Hello, Rus! What have you got there?"

"A birthday cake," replied Mr. Riley. "What have you got?"

"A birthday cake," said Mr. Davis. "I found it on top of the mailbox. Where did yours come from?"

"From the bakery," said Mr. Riley. "I thought that one was lost." He looked from one box to the other. "Well," he said, "I guess the first grade will have enough birthday cake."

The mailman and the bus driver went to the door of the first grade. It was just twelve o'clock. Miss Adams and all the children looked at the two men standing in the doorway, each holding a large box. "Here is Jonny's birthday cake," said Mr. Riley. "Only now it is birthday cakes."

"Oh, do stay and join the party!" said Miss Adams.

"Thanks!" said the bus driver and the mailman in a chorus.

So Mr. Davis and Mr. Riley stayed for Jonathan's birthday party and they all ate cake, not once, but twice. It was the first time Jonathan had had two birthday cakes. Everybody in the first grade thought it was a very good idea.

Three

Fourth of July Birthday

Billy Porter was born on the Fourth of July. By the time Billy was six, he had decided that the Fourth of July was a fine day but not a day for a birthday; for Billy liked birthday parties especially because of birthday presents. Who doesn't! Unfortunately, he soon found out that on the Fourth of July, most of his friends were too busy with celebration activities to attend a birthday party. Skinny Tucker was always busy being Uncle Sam in the Fourth of July parade. Skinny was always Uncle Sam because he was tall and thin and owned the right costume and a false beard. Betsy was always Betsy Ross in the parade because her name was Betsy. Kenny Roberts, who lived next door to Billy, was always busy on the Fourth of July decorating his bicycle to ride in the parade. On other days Kenny frequently let Billy ride on the bicycle. In fact Kenny had taught Billy to ride, but on the Fourth of July, Kenny was not lending his bicycle to anyone. Kenny liked to show off as he rode past the people who gathered to watch the parade. Kenny's favorite trick was "no hands," which meant peddling with his hands off the handlebars. He liked to hear people call out, "Hey, look at Kenny."

Friends who were not in the parade were usually off on family picnics. With no one able to come to his birthday party, there were no birthday presents, so there was nothing for Billy to do but walk in the parade, *tramp, tramp, tramp* until his feet were ready to drop off. Billy considered his birthday on the Fourth of July a bust.

The year that Billy was seven years old, the

day dawned bright and hot. When Billy sat down to breakfast, his mother said, "Happy birthday, Billy."

"Thanks," said Billy. "Same old Fourth of July! No party!"

"Now, don't be so gloomy," said his mother. "Here's your birthday present, right outside the door." Mrs. Porter opened the back door and Billy stepped out.

"Oh!" cried Billy, "Oh! A two-wheel bike! Oh! That's the greatest. Oh, thanks!"

Billy thought he had never seen a more beautiful bicycle. Red, white and blue paper had been woven into the wheels and a small American flag was flying from the handlebars. It looked exactly like Kenny Roberts's bike.

"Now!" said his mother. "I hope this will make up for not having a party."

"Oh yes!" said Billy. "Now I can ride in the parade, just like Kenny Roberts does."

Later in the morning, Betsy arrived at Billy's house. "Oh, Betsy," Billy cried, "come and see what I got for my birthday!"

When Betsy saw the bicycle, she said, "Gee,

Billy, it's the nicest bike I've ever seen, 'specially with all the decorations on it. Can you ride it?"

"Can I ride it!" Billy echoed. "I'm an expert. I learned to ride on Kenny's bike. Of course, if I could have a birthday party, I'd have a lot of presents. But the Fourth of July's a rotten day for being born!"

"Yes," said Betsy. "Like Star being born on Christmas."

"Oh, Star does all right," said Billy. "She gets a birthday tree with stars all over it! But there's no such thing as a Fourth of July tree."

Betsy laughed. "No, just the cherry tree they say George Washington chopped down when he was a kid."

Billy laughed. "Bet he didn't have a party on his birthday!"

"Guess not," said Betsy. "We're going to have supper in our backyard, and I've come over to invite you."

"Oh, that's great!" said Billy.

"Be sure to get there by half-past five," Betsy said. "Don't be late!"

Billy decided that a backyard picnic would make the Fourth of July a little better. And also, there was the new bicycle to ride in the parade.

At two o'clock, Billy, on his bicycle, joined the parade. He had never felt so proud. Wheeling along on his beautiful new bicycle, he felt like a king. He was glad he had practiced riding on Kenny Roberts's bike. Now, as Billy pedaled along, he heard some of his friends and neighbors call out, "Look, there goes Billy Porter on a new bike!" Billy felt so proud he decided to drive without using his hands. But just then a dog ran into the street, and Billy and the bicycle and the dog were suddenly all mixed up together.

A policeman came to the rescue and helped Billy up, while the dog ran off, yapping. Billy picked up his bicycle and dusted off the red, white and blue trimmings. Billy didn't feel so much like a king.

"I hope I didn't hurt the dog," he said.

"I don't think so," said the policeman. "But if I were you, I wouldn't try to show off. Keep your hands on the handlebars, or I'll give you a ticket for obstructing traffic." The policeman laughed. And Billy laughed, too.

In a moment he was on his bicycle and he quickly caught up to the parade. He began to feel very cocky. It was great to be riding such a beautiful bicycle, and soon he couldn't resist taking his hands off the handlebars once more. He beamed his widest grin at the people who were standing on the sidewalk, and he cried out, "See! No hands!" And he went *bump!* right into the side of the float on which Betsy Ross was busily sewing the American flag.

Billy fell with a thud off the bicycle right onto the end of Betsy's flag that was lying at her feet. As he tried to get up, he pulled the flag from Betsy's hands, and when he stood up he was draped in the American flag.

"Billy Porter!" cried Betsy. "What are you doing?"

"I fell off my bike," said Billy, trying to untangle himself from the flag.

At last Billy flung the flag back to Betsy and jumped off the float. He saw his bicycle lying near the gutter, and he reached it just as the policeman who had helped him up the first time he fell off arrived.

"So it's you again!" said the policeman. "Can't you ride that bike? Or were you doing that no-hands business again?"

Billy hung his head. "I guess so," he said.

"Well, if you do it again I'll turn you in," said the policeman. "You're a menace to the parade."

Billy looked up at the policeman and said, "You wouldn't really, would you?"

"Well, don't put me to the test," said the policeman. "Get along with you!"

Billy mounted his bicycle again and pedaled fast to catch up to the parade. He didn't try no hands again the rest of the afternoon.

Just before half-past five, Billy wheeled into Betsy's driveway and put his bicycle against the garage. As he walked back to the path that led to the backyard, he saw that the Japanese lanterns that Betsy's father hung up every year were already lighted.

"Gee," said Billy to himself. "Those lanterns

sure make it look like a party." And Billy wished again that he was having a birthday party.

Billy found Betsy standing beside the birdbath.

"Hi, Billy!" Betsy shouted, in a voice that could have been heard two blocks away. It made Billy jump. And suddenly, six children popped up from behind bushes and trees and cried out, "Surprise! Surprise! Happy birthday, Billy!"

Billy was so startled that he sat down suddenly on the grass. When he looked up, six of his friends were looking down at him, and each one was holding out a package. Then, as each one placed a package in Billy's hands, he or she said, "Happy birthday, Billy!"

Billy was so surprised it was hard for him to find his voice to say thank you. Soon the garden was strewn with wrapping paper as Billy opened his presents. There was a book from Kenny, a baseball from Richard, and a mitt from Richard's twin brother Henry. There was a T-shirt with "Tough Guy" on it from Betsy and many other nice gifts, such as games and puzzles.

The children played in the yard until six

o'clock, when Betsy's father came out and lit the outside grill. Soon he had hamburgers cooking, and then Betsy's mother brought out a dish of scalloped potatoes and a bowl of salad.

The children had a feast. And when they had finished, Betsy's mother brought out a large birthday cake with Billy's name written across it in blue icing. There were red candles.

Now everyone sang "Happy Birthday" to Billy. And then they all stood up and sang "The Star Spangled Banner."

"This is a real Fourth of July birthday party, isn't it, Billy?" asked Betsy.

"Sure is!" said Billy. "I'll never again say that the Fourth of July is a bad day for a birthday."

Four

Jennifer's Birthday

Jennifer would be seven years old tomorrow. She was an only child. She lived with her father and mother and two cocker spaniels, Davey and Sissy. Davey was black with a white bib under his nose, and Sissy was honey-colored. They were from the same litter and had been born on Jennifer's birthday, so every year Jennifer and Davey and Sissy celebrated their birthdays with cake and candles. It was always frosted with white icing with their names, Jennifer, Davey and Sissy, in pink icing.

The little dogs were Jennifer's playmates and meant more to her than her dolls because they were alive and returned her love and affection. Sometimes she dressed them up in her dolls' clothes and bonnets and took them for a walk in the dolls' baby carriage. She loved the licks the little dogs gave her in return for the kisses she placed on their heads. Every day when she came home from school they would rush to the door to meet her and she would have a romp with Davey and Sissy. Both of the dogs slept on the foot of Jennifer's bed and they kept her feet warm in cold weather.

Tonight when Jennifer gave the little dogs their good-night pats she said, "Tomorrow is our very own day 'cause it's your birthday and mine. Oh! It will be such a happy, happy day!"

Jennifer climbed into her little white bed and pushed her feet down under the covers. Feeling the dogs at her feet she felt cozy but for a long time she lay awake thinking of tomorrow, of the presents her father and mother would have for her, of the packages the mailman would bring from Grandmother and Aunt Grace and of the birthday cake with candles. She could almost smell the cake. Perhaps Mommy was making it now in the kitchen! Jennifer wiggled her toes with delight. She decided that her birthday was even more important than Christmas. Christmas belonged to everybody, but her birthday just belonged to her and to Davey and Sissy. At last, with a smile on her face, Jennifer fell asleep.

The next morning everything was just as it had been on other birthday mornings. She put on her new dress. Her birthday dress. Then she tied a blue ribbon on Davey's collar and a pink one on Sissy's. Then, followed by the two dogs, she ran downstairs where her mother and father hugged and kissed her. There were flowers on the breakfast table. "Just for your birthday," said her mother.

"Oh, lovely!" said Jennifer. "And tonight there will be birthday cake and ice cream for dinner, and my presents."

Her father took her face in his hands and said,

"Don't be too sure—the mailman may be taking a holiday because it's your birthday."

Jennifer laughed. "You're teasing me, Daddy. I'm not George Washington," she said. As she ran out the door she cried out, "Oh, it's a wonderful day!"

When Jennifer came home from school, she rushed into the house, calling out, "Oh Mommy! Mommy! It's been such a lovely day. Everybody sang 'Happy Birthday' to me in school this morning, and the girls all liked my birthday dress."

Mother was in the kitchen preparing dinner. Jennifer ran back and forth, in one room and then in another looking for the little dogs. "Mommy! Mommy!" she called out. "Where are the dogs? I can't find them. They didn't come to meet me, as they always do. I thought maybe they were hiding just for fun, but I've looked in all their favorite hiding places and I can't find them. Where do you suppose they are?"

"They must still be out," said her mother. "They were scratching at the door right after lunch, and I let them out for a run. They are a long time coming back, the little rascals."

Jennifer opened the back door and called, "Here, Davey! Here, Sissy!" The dogs did not appear.

"Don't worry," said her mother. "They'll be back, wanting their supper. Go upstairs now and wash your face and hands. I'm glad to see that you kept your dress clean for dinner tonight."

Jennifer ran upstairs and washed her face and hands. Then she ran to the head of the stairs and called down to her mother, "Mommy, I think I hear the dogs. I think they're at the front door. Please go see."

Jennifer looked over the stair railing and saw her mother go to the front door. Jennifer listened for the happy barks of Davey and Sissy, but no sound came. The dogs had not returned.

Jennifer went downstairs slowly. She was troubled about Davey and Sissy. They had always been free to run around the neighborhood, but they had never stayed out long. They always seemed glad to get back home to Jennifer.

At half-past four, Jennifer's father came home from his office. As soon as Jennifer heard his key in the lock, she ran to meet him. When the door opened, she said, "Oh, Daddy! Davey and Sissy must be lost. Mommy says they've been out a long time, and they haven't come back for their supper."

"Well, don't worry about them, dearie," said her father. "They know where they live. They always come back."

"But it's such a long time," said Jennifer. "Mommy says they went out right after lunch."

Jennifer's father sat down and took her on his lap, for he could see by her face that she was very worried. "Now, cheer up, darling. It's your birthday," he said. "Would you feel better," he continued, "if I drove around the neighborhood to see if I could find them?"

"Oh, yes, Daddy, and I'll come with you," Jennifer replied.

"Very well," said her father. "Go tell your mother that we're going out to look for the dogs."

Jennifer went off to the kitchen, but she was back in a minute, and said, "Mommy said not to worry about the time. We're having chicken and she can keep it hot until we come back."

"Good," said her father, "and birthday cake. Don't forget that. Now, let's get going. I don't think the dogs are very far away."

"Oh, Daddy," said Jennifer, as her father opened the door of the car for her. "You don't think they've been stolen, do you?"

"I don't think so," said her father. "Davey and Sissy would put up a fight if anyone tried to take them."

Jennifer's father drove slowly up one street and down another. Every once in a while he would stop and call loudly, "Here, Davey! Here, Sissy!" But the dogs did not respond. Once a big golden retriever came out of a yard and stood staring at the car. Then he barked several times before he returned to his yard.

After driving around the streets of the neighborhood, Jennifer's father reached the main highway that ran through the town. It led through a new development in which curbing and pavements had just been laid. There were a few new houses far apart. Jennifer's father continued to drive slowly and call out from time to time, "Here, Davey! Here, Sissy!"

The sun had gone down but there was still a glow from the sunset.

"Oh, why did they get lost?" moaned Jennifer. "Maybe we'll never find them."

"Now, don't worry," said her father. "I'm sure we'll find them." Her father drove on, stopping from time to time to call out the names of the dogs.

Suddenly Jennifer cried, "Oh, Daddy! I think I see them, way up the street! They are so far away they look like little toy dogs. Oh, Daddy, I'm sure it's Sissy and Davey."

Jennifer's father shaded his eyes with his hand and looked up the street. "I think you're right, Jennie," he said. "You do have sharp eyes." Her father stepped on the gas and drove faster. When he was near the dogs, he stopped.

The dogs were by the curb. Sissy was sitting beside Davey, who was lying close to the curb. Sissy did not run to the car, as she usually did, and Jennifer's father said, "That's very strange. The dogs know the car. They always come to the car." Then he put his arm around Jennifer's shoulder and said, "You stay right there, Jennie. I'll go to the dogs."

"No, no!" said Jennifer. "I'm coming."

As soon as Jennifer's father stepped out of the car, Jennifer saw Sissy get up. But Sissy didn't rush up with her usual happy yelps. She came whimpering and then she ran back to Davey.

"Something's the matter with Davey, Daddy," said Jennifer. "Something's the matter with him."

"Oh, Jennifer, do get back in the car," said her father. "I'll see to Davey."

"No, Daddy, no," said Jennifer. "Davey's my dog, and I want to see him." Jennifer got out of the car and followed her father to the curb where Davey was lying. Together they leaned over, and Jennifer's father placed his hand on Davey.

"Oh, Daddy, is he badly hurt?" said Jennifer, picking up Sissy.

Jennifer's father put his arm around Jennifer and said, "Darling, I'm afraid Davey has been hit by a car. I'm afraid he's dead. And dear little Sissy has been sitting beside him all the time."

Jennifer leaned her head on her father's shoulder. "Oh, no," she sobbed. "He can't be dead, Daddy. My Davey can't be dead. Oh, Daddy, Daddy, make him come alive, Daddy."

"I wish I could, darling," said her father. "I wish I could."

Jennifer's father picked up Davey and said, "Come, dear, get back in the car. We'll take him home." Her father carried the dog to the car. "I'll put him in the trunk," he said.

"Oh, no," sobbed Jennifer. "I want to hold him."

"Oh, darling, he's very dirty, and you may get blood on your nice dress."

"I don't care about my dress," she screamed. "I want to carry my Davey."

"Very well," said her father, picking up his newspaper. "I'll put this newspaper under him before I set him on your lap."

Her father placed the newspaper on her lap, and Jennifer held out her arms for Davey. Sissy jumped into the car and sat on the floor beside Jennifer. She didn't seem to want to be separated from Davey.

Jennifer continued to sob. "Somebody in a car killed Davey, didn't he?" she asked.

"Yes, he did," her father replied. "I guess whoever did it put Davey by the curb so that he wouldn't be hit by another car."

As her tears fell on Davey, she said, "But why didn't they take him to a vet?" Jennifer was sobbing now. "Why didn't they phone us? Our telephone number is on the dog tag. It was a wicked, wicked person who killed my Davey."

Jennifer's father gathered her close and said, "We don't know how it happened, dear. Maybe the driver couldn't stop."

"He stopped to put Davey by the curb," said Jennifer, wiping tears out of her eyes. "He could have taken Davey to a vet."

Jennifer's tears fell on Davey's glossy fur. She had petted him since his puppy days. Now he was stiff and cold. Jennifer cried all the way home. People in passing cars heard her and wondered what could be the matter with the little girl.

When Jennifer and her father reached home, her father pulled a reluctant Sissy out of the car.

Then he took Davey out of Jennifer's arms and Jennifer, still sobbing, followed her father into the house. Then she ran to her mother and cried, "Oh, Mommy! Somebody killed Davey! On his birthday they killed him."

Jennifer's mother gathered her little girl into her arms and now both Jennifer and her mother cried. When her father came in, he told her mother how they found the two dogs, Sissy sitting beside her brother.

"I guess she sat beside him all afternoon," Jennifer sobbed. "Sissy loved him so much."

"Yes," said her father. "She would never have left him." This made Jennifer cry harder.

Her mother smoothed her mussed-up dress. "Come," she said, "dinner is ready."

Jennifer said, "Never mind, Mommy. I don't want any dinner."

"But there is a beautiful birthday cake and there are presents to open."

"I can't eat birthday cake and I don't want to open presents now that my Davey is dead."

Jennifer's father patted Jennifer and said, "I'm

going to take Davey now to Dr. Sam, the nice vet, and he will bury Davey in the doggie cemetery that he has."

Jennifer cried and cried.

When she heard her father start his car, Jennifer sobbed, "Now I'll never see my Davey again."

Jennifer's mother tried to comfort her, but now Jennifer felt tired and sick. She was afraid she was going to be sick all over her new dress, and she didn't care. Davey was gone, her precious Davey.

Neither Jennifer nor her parents could eat any dinner. And even Sissy turned away from her supper dish and crawled under the sofa.

The birthday cake sat untouched in the kitchen.

Jennifer's father hadn't been back very long when the front doorbell rang. He went to the door and Jennifer heard him say, "Yes, come in. Yes, Davey was our dog. He was my little girl's dog. I think you should talk to her."

When Jennifer heard this, she slid off the sofa and ran to the kitchen, where her mother was putting the food away. "Mommy!" Jennifer cried,

"I don't want to see that man! He's a wicked man! He killed my Davey!"

Now her father had come into the kitchen. "Come, Jennifer," he said. "The man is very, very sorry it happened, and he wants to tell you how sorry he is."

"I won't go see him," said Jennifer. "He's a wicked man. He didn't try to save Davey's life. He didn't take him to the vet." Jennifer was sobbing again.

"Come now, Jennie," said her father. "The man is sorry, and he wants to tell you how it happened."

Now Jennifer let her father lead her back to the living room. Then the man came to her and knelt down beside her. "Honey," he said, "I can't tell you how terrible I feel about Davey."

Jennifer began to cry very hard once more.

The man continued. "You see, I was taking my wife to the hospital because our baby was about to be born. My wife was in great pain. I was hurrying to get her to the hospital as fast as possible. As I approached the two cocker spaniels, I saw the black one run out onto the street. He ran by the wheels of the car, barking. And suddenly he ran right in front of the car. I couldn't avoid hitting him."

"Why didn't you take him to a vet?" Jennifer sobbed.

"I had to get my wife to the hospital," said the man. "I only had time to carry Davey to the curb. I didn't want another car to hit him. I just took time to write down your address and telephone number. When I drove away, the little tan dog was sitting beside Davey. Now I have come to tell you how sorry I am. I want to give you another little dog just like Davey."

"No, no!" Jennifer cried. "If I can't have Davey, I don't want another one. I don't want it."

"Perhaps you will feel better about it later, and I'll take you to get a new puppy," said the man, as he offered Jennifer his pocket handkerchief to dry her tears.

Jennifer hiccupped and said, "Did you get a little baby?"

"Yes, indeed," said the man. "A nice baby boy. And we named him David."

Jennifer's eyes opened wide, and she said, "Davey?"

"No, David," said the baby's father. "Perhaps you'll come to see him. We live nearby."

The next day the man telephoned. Jennifer's mother answered, and when she hung up the receiver she said to Jennifer, "That was the father of the new baby. He and his wife have invited us to attend the christening of David on Sunday morning. They would like you to hold the baby."

"Oh, Mommy!" cried Jennifer. "Really, truly?"

"That's what he said," said her mother.

"Oh, I'd love to hold the baby," said Jennifer. "But what would I wear?"

"I'll wash and iron your birthday dress," said her mother, "and it will look beautiful."

When Sunday came, Jennifer walked with her father and mother to the church for the christening. There the young mother placed the baby in Jennifer's arms and Jennifer held him close while the water was put on the baby's head and he was christened David. Then Jennifer looked down on the little boy and whispered, "Hello, little Davey."

Five

The Cake and the Crown

Whenever students in Mrs. Wilkins's first-grade class had a birthday, they celebrated with a make-believe cake with real candles. It was made of a round cardboard box covered with something that looked like yellow icing. When it not was being used, it was kept on a plate under a glass cover. Because it never got dusty, it always looked like a freshly baked birthday cake. Although it couldn't be eaten, the birthday boy or girl enjoyed blowing out the yellow candles. Then all the children ate what they called birthday cookies.

The make-believe birthday cake was often borrowed by other classes in the school. Sometimes they forgot to return it. Then when a first-grade child was having a birthday, the whole school had to be searched to find the birthday cake.

One day, when Mrs. Wilkins needed a long time to find the birthday cake, she said, "If we just had an oven, we could bake our birthday cakes."

The following Monday morning Bruce rushed into the room and said to Mrs. Wilkins, "I've brought a present! Daddy is bringing it in."

"Oh, Bruce!" Mrs. Wilkins exclaimed. "It isn't another cage with an animal, is it?"

"No!" Bruce answered. "It's just what you wanted. It's an oven! We got a new one at our home, and my father said I could bring the old one to school. I told my father you would like it."

"An oven!" exclaimed Mrs. Wilkins. "How big is the oven?"

"Oh, it's big enough to roast a turkey," Bruce

replied. "My mother roasted turkeys in it."

Just then Bruce's father appeared at the door with the oven. The big electric cord hung down like a tail. Mrs. Wilkins was glad to see that the oven was not as big as a rabbit's cage. "See!" said Bruce. "It's big enough to roast a turkey."

"Why, Mr. Cramer!" said Mrs. Wilkins. "How nice of you to bring us an oven! I'll clear off a table, so that you can put it down."

As Mrs. Wilkins cleared a table, the children watched and asked questions. "Are we going to cook a turkey, Mrs. Wilkins? When can we cook? Will we get pots and pans?"

At last Bruce's father placed the oven on the table. "Well, have fun!" he said to Mrs. Wilkins.

"Thank you very much," said Mrs. Wilkins. "This is a very fine present. Now we shall all learn to cook."

As Bruce's father left the room, he laughed and said, "I hope I'll be invited to eat some of the cooking."

"Indeed, we won't forget you," Mrs. Wilkins replied.

When the door closed, Chuckie said, "See if it works. Maybe it doesn't work."

"'Course it works!" said Bruce. "My father wouldn't give us an oven that didn't work."

Bruce plugged the cord into the nearest outlet. The children gathered around the oven. When they saw two rods inside turn from black to bright orange, they shouted, "It works!"

Christie clapped her hands and said, "Oh, Mrs. Wilkins! Now we can make real birthday cakes!"

"Oh, yes!" the children cried. "Real birthday cakes! How soon can we make a birthday cake?"

"My birthday is next Friday," said Debbie.

"Oh! Debbie!" said Christie. "You'll have the first real birthday cake, and we'll all bake it for you. What kind do you want?"

Debbie stood with her finger in her mouth. She was thinking. At last she said, "I want one with yellow icing and yellow candles."

Christie turned to Mrs. Wilkins and said, "Can Debbie have a cake with yellow icing and yellow candles?"

"Indeed, she can," Mrs. Wilkins replied. "We'll make it for her on Thursday afternoon."

"Why not Friday morning?" Mark asked. "Why do we have to make it Thursday afternoon?"

"Because we go to assembly on Friday morning," Mrs. Wilkins replied. "A third-grade class is going to have a play. There wouldn't be time to bake a cake on Friday morning."

"I can't wait to help bake that cake," said Margie.

Mrs. Wilkins gathered the children around her. "Come," she said, "come sit, on the floor. I'm going to read you a story."

The children settled down on the floor, but before Mrs. Wilkins had time to open the book Margie raised her hand.

"What is it?" Mrs. Wilkins asked.

Margie stood up and faced the other children. "It's about birthdays. At our house we wear a crown on our birthday. Whoever has a birthday wears a crown all day long."

"Can we make a crown, Mrs. Wilkins?" Christie asked.

"I think so," Mrs. Wilkins replied. "After I read the story, I'll try to make a crown."

Margie sat down, and Mrs. Wilkins began to read. On other days the children always chatted about the story. Today, as soon as the story was finished, the children only wanted to talk about the crown.

"It must be a gold crown," said Margie.

"I'll see if I have some gold cardboard," said Mrs. Wilkins, pulling open a closet door. She looked through one of the shelves, and soon the children saw her pull out a piece of gold cardboard.

"It must have points all around the top," said Bruce. "Crowns always have five points around the top."

Mrs. Wilkins laid the sheet of cardboard on a table. Then she said, "I'll have to measure Debbie's head, so it will be the right size." Mrs. Wilkins looked around for Debbie. "Where is she?" she asked.

"She went to get a drink of water," Christie replied.

Bruce was standing next to her, so Mrs. Wilkins said, "Come, Bruce, I'll measure your head." With a tape measure, she measured Bruce's head. Then she marked off the inches on the cardboard with a ruler.

"Can I make the points?" Philip asked. Philip was very proud of being the best artist in the class.

"You can make the points," Mrs. Wilkins replied.

After Philip had drawn the edge of the crown, Mrs. Wilkins let Christie cut it out with the scissors. Then she fastened the back of the crown with paper clips. "Now, Bruce," she said, "try on the crown," Mrs. Wilkins placed the crown on Bruce's head and it fit nicely.

By this time Debbie was back. "May I try it on?" she asked. "Since I'm going to be the first one to wear it."

Bruce took it off and put it on Debbie's head. It went down over Debbie's ears and sat like a collar around her neck, for Debbie was a very small girl. Everyone laughed.

"That will never do!" said Mrs. Wilkins. "We shall have to fit the crown for each wearer with paper clips." When Mrs. Wilkins had changed the position of the paper clips, Debbie could wear the crown.

"Debbie will be the first birthday princess," said Christie.

"Next month I'll be a birthday king," said Philip.

"And we'll have to move the paper clips again," said Chuckie.

The following Thursday Christie met Mrs. Wilkins at the school yard gate. Mrs. Wilkins was carrying a parcel. "We're going to bake the birthday cake today, aren't we?" Christie asked.

"I have a box of cake mix in this parcel," Mrs. Wilkins replied. "And three eggs."

"What about the yellow candles?" Christie asked.

"I have a box of candles in my desk," Mrs. Wilkins answered.

In the afternoon, when Mrs. Wilkins asked Bruce to plug in the oven, all the children were excited about baking their first birthday cake.

Christie brought out the clean mixing bowl.

Sara opened the box of cake mix.

Mark measured a half-cup of water.

Philip asked if he could break the eggs. He broke one into the bowl and the other on the floor. "Oops! Sorry about that!" he said. "If my cat were here, he'd eat it. My cat loves eggs. We need a cat, Mrs. Wilkins. Don't you think we need a cat?"

"We need another rabbit!" said Margie. "We need a papa rabbit. Then we would have baby rabbits."

"I think we need a cat," said Philip.

"We do not need a cat," said Mrs. Wilkins. "We just need someone who can break eggs into the bowl."

"Let me do it! I can do it!" came from every child.

"Mark, you do it!" said Mrs. Wilkins. "I only brought three eggs. If you drop the one that is left, we can't make the cake."

Mark held his breath as he picked up the egg. "Oh, be careful," said Christie.

"Don't crack it hard!" said Margie.

The rest of the children were holding their breath.

"Stop bugging me!" said Mark, as he cracked the egg against the edge of the bowl.

"Oh, the eggshell went in!" Philip cried out. "The eggshell's in!"

As Mark fished the eggshell out of the bowl, he said, "Well, I got the egg into the bowl."

Then Mrs. Wilkins beat the batter while the children watched. As she poured it into the shiny cake pan, the children murmured, "Yummy! Yummy!"

As soon as the cake was in the oven, the children started watching the clock. They spent most of the next hour running to look through the glass window in the door of the oven. At last the cake was done, but it had to cool before the yellow icing could be smoothed over it.

Mrs. Wilkins put the make-believe cake on the top shelf of the closet. "Now that we have a real birthday cake we don't need the make-believe one," she said, as she locked the closet door.

By the time the children left at the end of the day, the cake had been frosted. The beautiful yellow birthday cake with seven yellow candles was left standing on the same plate where the make-believe cake had always stood. It was covered with the same glass cover. The gold crown was resting on the top of the glass cover. Everything was ready for Debbie's birthday the next morning.

The following morning Debbie was surrounded by her friends. They met Mrs. Wilkins at the front door and followed her to their room. As they entered the room, Christie called out, "Now Debbie must put on her crown."

"Yes, indeed!" said Mrs. Wilkins. "Come, put on your birthday crown." Mrs. Wilkins led Debbie to the table where she had left the cake and the crown. The table was empty. "Why, where are they?" Mrs. Wilkins exclaimed. She looked all around the room. "Where can they be?" she asked.

The children were speechless. Mrs. Wilkins dashed out of the room. As each child came into the room, he was told, "The birthday cake's gone, and the crown is gone, too."

When Mrs. Wilkins returned, the children saw

that her hands were empty. She said to the children, "No one on this floor knows anything about our birthday cake or the crown. The office doesn't know anything about them either."

The children's faces looked very sad, and Debbie was close to tears.

"I'm sure we'll find that everything is quite safe," said Mrs. Wilkins, trying to bring some cheer to the children. "We must go to the assembly now. We don't want to be late for the play."

Mrs Wilkins's children marched into the assembly hall. Not a single face was smiling. They sat down and looked at the drawn curtains on the stage. They joined in the opening song, but their voices were very weak. No one felt like singing.

When the song ended, a boy from the third grade stepped from between the curtains and said, "This play that we are about to present is called *The King's Birthday*."

The first graders pricked up their ears and sat up.

The curtains opened, and there sat a boy in a long royal robe, wearing the gold crown that

Debbie should have been wearing. In front of him, on a table, was the birthday cake that Mrs. Wilkins and her class had made the day before. The children pointed to the cake and whispered to each other, "That's our cake! That's our cake!"

Debbie didn't listen to a word that the children on the stage were speaking. She just thought about her crown and her birthday cake. The play went on and on. Debbie thought it would never end.

At last the children heard the king say, "And now I shall cut my birthday cake."

Mrs. Wilkins's class stood up and cried out, "Don't cut it!"

Debbie shouted as loud as she could, "That's my birthday cake and that's my crown!"

The children on stage were so surprised that they didn't know what to do. Children all over the room stood up to see what was the matter with Mrs. Wilkins's first grade. Debbie's big sister called out, "That's my little sister's birthday cake!"

Everyone was glad when the curtain closed on

the king and his subjects and the birthday cake.

When Mrs. Wilkins's class returned to their room, Mrs. Garvey, who taught third grade, was standing by the door. She was holding the birthday cake and the crown. "I'm sorry!" she said. "I sent one of the boys to borrow the make-believe cake that you have always loaned us. We didn't know that it was a real cake until the children called out to us."

Debbie and all of the children were happy again. Debbie wore her gold crown, and the children sang, "Happy birthday, dear Debbie, happy birthday to you." When they ate the birthday cake, they knew it was real. They all agreed that it was yummy!

Six

The Wettest Birthday Ever

Robin was having a party on his sixth birthday. Six boys from the first grade had been invited. Robin could hardly wait for the day to come. Every morning he said to his mother, "How many days to my birthday party? Say it like they do for the space blast-off."

So his mother counted down, each day getting nearer to zero.

"When it's zero," said Robin every day, "I'll say bang! Like the rocket when it goes off."

Robin also looked forward to the birthday presents that he hoped to receive. "I guess I'll get a book to color from Brucie, 'cause everybody thinks coloring books are birthday presents."

"That will be nice," said his mother. "You like books to color."

"Sure," Robin replied, "but I'd rather have a boat to sail in the bathtub."

"You have a boat," said his mother.

"It's just a little boat," said Robin. "I would like a bigger boat. You know, Mommy. A real boaty boat!"

"Wait and see," said his mother.

One day Robin said to his mother, "Will we play games at my birthday party?"

"Yes," his mother replied. "I have decided to take you and your friends to the park, where you can play games."

"Is that the park where the ducks are?" Robin asked.

"That's the place!" his mother replied.

"Oh!" said Robin. "It will be a picnic birthday party, won't it?"

"Not exactly," said his mother.

"Not just sandwiches and no birthday cake or ice cream?" Robin asked.

"Oh, of course there will be a birthday cake and ice cream," said his mother.

"With a sparkler or candles?" Robin asked.

"Which do you like best?" his mother asked.

"Candles, because I like to blow them out," said Robin. "But how can you have a cake with candles on a picnic?" Robin asked.

"Oh, we'll have our ice cream and cake before we go to the park to play games."

The day finally arrived when Robin called out "Bang!" and shouted, "It's my birthday!"

"Yes," said his mother. "Happy birthday!"

"What time is the party?" Robin asked.

"At two o'clock," his mother replied.

"When is two o'clock?" Robin asked.

"After lunch," his mother replied.

"I wonder what the birthday presents will be?" Robin said again and again.

"I'm sure they will be very nice," said his mother.

Shortly before two o'clock, Robin's friend Brucie arrived. He handed a flat package to Robin and said, "Happy birthday, Robin."

"Thank you," Robin replied. As he ripped off the wrapping paper, he said, "Bet it's a coloring book!"

Brucie laughed.

Sure enough, it was a coloring book. Robin carried it to his mother. "Look, Mommy," he said. "Brucie brought me a coloring book."

"How very nice," said his mother. "What fun you'll have coloring all of those pictures."

"Oh, yes," said Robin. "I like to color pictures."

A few minutes later Christopher arrived. He, too, gave Robin a flat parcel. "Happy birthday, Robbie!" he said.

Robin ripped off the paper and found his present. "Look, Mommy," he called. "Chris brought me a coloring book!"

"Isn't that nice," said his mother. "Now you'll have a lot of pictures to color."

"Yes," said Robin. "A lot!"

When Robin's friend Jamie arrived, he handed Robin a package and said, "Happy birthday!"

Robin saw that Jamie's present was also flat, but he still hoped for a surprise. But there again in his hand was another coloring book. Robin stared down at the book.

"Do you like it, Robbie?" Jamie asked.

"Oh, sure. Thanks," said Robin as he placed it on top of the other two books.

The next boy to arrive was Andy. As he came through the door, he said, "Happy birthday, Robbie! I brought you a present."

Robin took the parcel and said, "Thanks." But he didn't like the way it felt. He carried it to his mother and said, "Here, Mommy. You open it for me."

"You should open your own birthday present," said his mother. "Don't you want to open it?"

"No," said Robin. "You open it."

His mother opened the parcel while Robin looked on anxiously. "Why, it's a coloring book," said his mother. "Isn't that nice, Robin."

"Uh-huh," said Robin.

"What fun you'll have coloring all those pictures," said his mother.

"Uh-huh," said Robin.

In a short time Ray arrived. Robin could see that Ray was carrying a flat parcel. He was grinning broadly as he handed it to Robin and said, "Happy birthday."

"Is it a coloring book?" Robin asked.

The grin faded from Ray's face. "Oh, I'm sorry!" he said. "Did you want a coloring book? If I had known you wanted a coloring book, I would have brought you a coloring book. I'm sorry."

"Don't be sorry," said Robin, "I have a lot of coloring books, I just thought you had brought me one."

"I hope you like what I brought you," said Ray.

"Oh, I'll like it!" said Robin, as he tore the paper off the parcel. When Robin opened it he found it was a game. "Oh, that's great! Thank you," said Robin. Ray's grin returned.

In a few minutes his friend Jack arrived. Robin looked at Jack, expecting to see another flat parcel sticking out from under Jack's arm. But there was no flat parcel under Jack's arm. Instead, he was carrying what looked like a box.

"Happy birthday!" said Jack, and he handed the parcel to Robin.

Robin took the parcel in both hands. "Oh, thanks!" he said. "Thanks."

Robin sat down and began picking at the bow of ribbon that was tied in a knot. "I bet this is something good!" he said.

"Sure it is," said Jack. "My daddy took me to buy it. You know my daddy's in the navy."

"Sure, I know," said Robin with wide eyes. "I think the navy's wonderful when they play football. Especially when they bring the goat. That's the mascot," he said to all of the boys in the room. "I would like to be in the navy when I grow up."

Now Robin had the ribbon off. Frantically he ripped off paper and looked down at the box. Robin could hardly wait to lift the lid, for on the lid was a picture of a boat. "Oh!" cried Robin. "I bet it's a boat!"

"You just look inside," said Jack.

Robin was so excited he could hardly lift the lid.

"Here, I'll help you," said Jack.

"No! No!" Robin cried. "I can do it! I can do it!" Now Robin was off the chair and jumping up and down with excitement. But in a few minutes he was quiet enough to open the box. There, to his delight, was a boat.

It was painted gray. "It's a navy ship," said Jack.

"Oh, it's great," said Robin, as the other boys in the room gathered around him.

"Ooooh!" they said in a chorus. "Look at that boat!"

Robin ran with the boat to his mother. "Look, Mommy!" he said. "Look what Jack brought me! It's a boat—a navy boat!"

Robin's mother took the boat in her hands. "What a beautiful boat it is," she said. And to Jack, she said, "Jack, your father must have picked this out."

Jack beamed. "He did," he said.

"I'm going to see how it looks in the water," said Robin. "I'll float it in the bathtub."

Jack and the other boys followed Robin to the bathroom, and in a few minutes all seven boys were gathered around the bathtub, watching the water running into the tub. When the tub was filled, Robin placed the boat in the water, and all of the boys said, "Ooooh!"

Jack took hold of the top of the mast. "See!" he said. "It even has a crow's nest."

"I want to see the crow!" Brucie cried out. "Let me see the crow!"

"Are there any eggs in the nest?" Chris called out. "I never saw a crow's egg."

Jack laughed. "You kids don't know anything about ships. The crow's nest is where a sailor climbs in and looks out over the water for enemy ships."

Robin gave the boat a push, and the boys shouted, "There she goes!"

"I'm the captain of the ship," said Robin, "'cause it's mine."

"And I'm first mate," said Jack, "'cause I gave it to you. Right?"

"Sure," said Robin. Then, throwing out his hands, he said, "You other kids are the crew."

"I'm the one climbing up the mast to the crow's nest," said Brucie.

"No!" cried Chris, "I'm in the crow's nest! I'm looking out over the water with my spyglass! I'm looking for the enemy."

"You get out of the crow's nest," shouted Brucie, "'cause I'm the one that's going to do that!"

"You can't," said Chris, "'cause it's me that's in the crow's nest!"

"I'm climbing up the mast!" cried Brucie.

"No!" cried Chris, grabbing hold of Brucie. In a moment the two boys were wrestling and shouting. "It's me! It's me!"

Suddenly Brucie's foot slipped. He pushed Chris toward the side of the tub, and they both fell over into the water. There was a great splash that sent water all over the other boys.

"Mommy! Mommy!" cried Robin. "Come quick!"

Robin's mother rushed in and looked with surprise at the boys, dripping water all over the bathroom.

"Brucie and Chris had a fight," said Robin.

"But all of you are wet!" said his mother. "You must take off your shirts while I get some dry T-shirts for you to put on."

The boys took off their wet shirts and in a short time Robin's mother was back with some of Robin's T-shirts. She handed one to each boy. When they had put them on, his mother laughed when she saw each boy wearing a T-shirt with the name Robbie across his chest. She said, "Now that I have seven Robbies, I wonder which one is having a birthday party?"

Robin held up his hand and cried. "Me! When do we eat?"

Robin's mother led the boys to the table where a beautiful birthday cake with six lighted candles stood.

"I know where I sit," cried Robin, "I sit where the cake is! Oh boy! What a cake!"

The boys found their chairs and Christopher sat next to Robin.

Then Robin's mother placed a dish filled with ice cream in front of each boy.

Brucie turned to Robin and said, "Bet you can't blow out the candles in one puff."

"Watch me!" said Robin, filling out his chest and getting ready to blow. But just as he was about to blow, Christopher blew the candles out.

"Hey! Watcha do that for?" Robin cried out, striking Christopher a sharp blow on his shoulder. Christopher fell off his chair and landed on the floor.

"I was just helping you puff, and now you made me bump my head on the floor," said Christopher, as he brushed away a tear.

"I don't need anybody to help me blow out candles!" said Robin. "I can do my own huffing and puffing."

The boys around the table shouted gleefully, "He can huff and puff and blow the house in."

While everyone, even Robin and Christopher, laughed, they all watched Robin's mother light the candles again.

Robin looked around at his friends and said, "Now I'm going to blow them out by myself." But his friends were in a blowing mood. They all blew but only Robin's puff reached the candles, and they all went out at once.

Robin could see into the living room and he saw his mother sit down at the piano. The boys heard the music and they began to sing "Happy Birthday."

When the boys finished eating their ice cream and cake Robin's mother said, "Now we are going to the park to play games. Come along. Go out and get into the station wagon."

There was a great deal of scrambling to get into the car. At long last the seven boys were in the station wagon, wriggling and calling out, "Move over! I don't have enough room! I want to sit by the window. You're kicking me! You're sitting on my hand! Well, get your hand off the seat!"

"Boys, boys, settle down," said Robin's mother.

Suddenly there was a roll of thunder. "Oh, no," said Robin's mother. "I'm afraid we're going to have a storm."

In a few moments there was a terrible clap of thunder and it began to rain.

It was a short drive to the park, through tree-lined streets, down a steep hill, across a little bridge, and into an open area that bordered a creek. "Oh, there are the ducks!" cried Robin.

"Ducks!" shouted all of the boys.

Now the thunder seemed to be rolling away but it was still raining and Robin's mother said, "I can see the ground is going to be too wet to play games."

"I don't care," said Robin. "I want to see the ducks."

"Me, too!" said each boy.

Everyone stayed in the car until the rain stopped. Then they got out of the car and soon they were all at the edge of the creek, each boy pointing out his favorite duck.

Robin held up his fist and said, "I saved a bit of my birthday cake for my favorite duck and I'm going to give it to him." But when he looked for his favorite it was on the other side of the creek. Stepping-stones showed plainly in the water so Robin decided to cross the creek to get nearer the duck.

His mother called out, "Be careful, Robin! The water isn't deep but it is very wet."

"I know," said Robin, wobbling on a slippery stone.

Bruce called out, "Oh, Robbie, you're going to fall in the creek!"

"I'm O.K." said Robin, as both feet sank into the mud.

"Ooops!" Christopher cried out. "There goes Robbie!"

"I'm O.K.," Robin called back, as he dropped the piece of cake in front of the duck and watched the duck gobble it up.

At that very moment it began to rain again. "Boys!" cried Robin's mother. "Get back in the car! I haven't any more dry T-shirts." Then she added, "Come quickly, Robbie, and don't fall into the creek." Robin slithered over the stones as the other boys ran to the car.

At last, very wet, Robin reached the car. "Well, I didn't fall in the creek," he said.

"No," said his mother, "but you couldn't be any wetter than you are."

"But I fed my duck a piece of my birthday cake," said Robin.

Now Christopher called from the back of the car, "Can I have a piece of Robbie's birthday cake to take home to my mother?"

"Of course," said Robin's mother.

"Can I?" came from the other boys.

"Of course," said Robin's mother.

When the boys left they were each carrying a little bag with a piece of birthday cake for their mothers.

Standing at the front window, Robin watched his friends as they walked away. He saw Brucie licking his fingers and Christopher poking into his paper bag.

Robin laughed and wondered whether their mothers would get any birthday cake at all.

Seven

Mr. Kilpatrick's Birthday

It was a stormy March morning. Betsy was only half-awake but she could hear the rain beating against the windowpane. She turned over and buried her face in the pillow. Then she heard her mother's voice calling her.

"Time to get up!" Mother opened the door. "Come along, Betsy," she said. "It's a very stormy day."

"Mmm!" said Betsy, opening her eyes. "All right, Mother."

Her mother closed the door and Betsy sat up. She stared at the window. It looked as though a great giant were throwing tubfuls of water at the window. The wind rattled the glass and whistled around the corner of the house.

Betsy got out of bed and went to the window. She looked down into the yard, where in summer her mother had a garden. Now it was a great puddle, with here and there a dripping bush. The bare branches of the trees blew in the wind.

A car passed, throwing water as high as its windows. It was a bright red car and it reminded Betsy of Mr. Kilpatrick the policeman, who was the friend of all the children at school. He had been a very special friend of Betsy's ever since she had been in the first grade. Betsy remembered now that today was a very important day. It was Mr. Kilpatrick's birthday and the boys and girls in Betsy's class were having a birthday party for him, a surprise birthday party.

Betsy ran into the bathroom. She was glad she had taken a bath last night. She would be ready in a jiffy. She was in a hurry, for Mr. Kilpatrick's birthday present was not yet wrapped. Betsy had bought it yesterday at the dime store and she was pleased with it. She felt certain that Mr. Kilpatrick would be pleased, too. It was a shiny belt buckle with a design on it that Betsy thought looked just like the badge that Mr. Kilpatrick wore on his coat. The man who had sold it to Betsy said it was made especially for policemen. She had been delighted to find something so perfect for Mr. Kilpatrick.

Betsy ran downstairs as soon as she was dressed. She went into the kitchen where her mother was frying bacon.

"Good morning, Betsy," said her mother.

"Good morning, Mother," said Betsy. "Do you know what?"

"What?" said Mother.

"It's Mr. Kilpatrick's birthday," replied Betsy.

"He certainly picked a wet day," said her mother.

"Doesn't make any difference," said Betsy. "We're having the party indoors at lunchtime. Mr. Kilpatrick doen't know a thing about it. He'll be surprised, all right."

"Will there be a cake?" Mother asked.

"Of course!" said Betsy, picking up a glass of orange juice. "Billy Porter is bringing the cake. His mother baked it. Mrs. Porter makes wonderful cake with very gooey icing."

"Come sit down and eat your breakfast," said her mother, placing on the table a soft-boiled egg with bits of bacon floating around in it.

Betsy sat down and stirred her egg. "Where's Father?" she asked.

"Your father left very early today. He took the car," replied her mother.

"Then do I have to walk to school?" Betsy asked.

"I'll ask Mrs. Porter to stop for you," said her mother. "I don't imagine that Billy is walking to school with a birthday cake on a morning like this."

Mother went into the hall to telephone Mrs. Porter and Betsy ate her breakfast. When her mother returned she said, "Mrs. Porter says she'll be glad to pick you up."

"That's good," said Betsy, as she drank the last drop of cocoa.

As Betsy left the kitchen she said, "Mother, have you any very nice paper that I can use to wrap up Mr. Kilpatrick's birthday present?"

"I'll see," said her mother.

Mother looked in a closet and pulled out some pieces of paper. She put them on the hall table. "This is all I have," she said.

Betsy looked them over. The first one she picked up was white with Santa Claus in his sleigh dashing all over it. "Well, it isn't a Christmas present," said Betsy. "I can't use that."

The next piece was pale blue with the word *baby* written all over it in white. "This won't do either," said Betsy. "Mr. Kilpatrick isn't a baby. He's a great big policeman."

Betsy picked up a third sheet. It was pink with pictures of a baby's rattle all over it. "Oh, crumbs!" said Betsy. "More baby stuff."

Underneath was one last sheet. It had bright flags on it. "Now this is more like it!" cried Betsy. "This is just perfect for Mr. Kilpatrick."

Betsy wrapped up her little parcel and tied it with a piece of red ribbon that still had a Christmas tag hanging from it. Betsy took it off and tied a little card on the ribbon. She had written it the night before. It said, "Happy Birthday to Mr. Kilpatrick from Betsy."

"You didn't see what I bought for Mr. Kilpatrick, Mother," said Betsy.

"No, I didn't, dear," said her mother. "I was busy. What did you buy for him?"

"Oh, it's wonderful," said Betsy. "It's a belt buckle and it matches his policeman's badge. The man in the store said it was made specially. I had some money Gramp sent to me."

"How nice, Betsy!" said her mother. "Weren't you fortunate to find it?"

"I'll unwrap it and show it to you," said Betsy. But just as she was about to untie the ribbon, a horn sounded out front. "Oh, there they are!" Betsy cried, and she put the package into her schoolbag.

Mother opened the front door and called out, "Just a minute," while Betsy took her raincoat out of the closet.

In a minute Betsy was ready with raincoat, rubbers and umbrella. She picked up her schoolbag and kissed her mother good-bye. Her mother opened the front door and Betsy dashed out into the pouring rain.

"Hi!" shouted Billy Porter. "Get in the back, Betsy. There isn't room for you in front, because I've got Mr. Kilpatrick's birthday cake here on the seat."

Mrs. Porter reached back and opened the car door for Betsy. "Good morning, Betsy," she said, as Betsy climbed in.

"Good morning," said Betsy. "Thank you for coming for me."

"We couldn't have you walking to school in this rain," said Mrs. Porter.

"You ought to see the big puddles in the streets," said Billy. "Regular lakes."

Mrs. Porter took off the brake and drove up the street. Betsy stood up and looked over the back of the front seat. "Where's the birthday cake?" she asked.

"Right here on the seat between us," said Billy. Betsy looked down at the cardboard box. "It's big, isn't it?" she said.

"You should see it!" said Billy. "It's a swell

cake. It's got pink icing with 'Happy Birthday' in white across the top."

"Has it got candles?" asked Betsy.

"Not yet," replied Billy, "but I've got the candles in my pocket."

"We don't know how many candles to put on it," said Betsy, "because we don't know how old Mr. Kilpatrick is."

"Well, I've got two dozen," said Billy. "You can't get any more than twenty-four candles on the top of a cake anyway."

As Betsy sat on the back seat of the car, Billy shouted, "Oh, boy! Look at this flood ahead. It's a lake. Look at that car! It's throwing water as high as the roof."

Excited, Billy stood up to look at the big puddle of water. His mother swung the car as far away from the center of the puddle as possible. As she did so, the box with the birthday cake slid across the seat. At the same moment Billy sat down, kerplunk, right on the birthday cake.

"Oops!" cried Billy.

Mrs. Porter stopped the car by the curb and

Billy got off the birthday cake. Mrs. Porter covered her face with her hands. "I'm afraid to look," she said. Betsy was looking over the back of the seat again. She looked down at the smashed box. Billy lifted the lid and peeked inside. "I guess I sort of knocked it out of shape," he said.

Mrs. Porter took her hands from her eyes and looked at the cake. It was indeed out of shape. It was broken into a great many pieces and some of them were very flat. Most of the pink icing was sticking to the inside of the lid. "What a mess!" exclaimed Mrs. Porter.

"I don't know how it happened," said Billy.

"You just sat on it," said his mother.

"Oh, no!" exclaimed Billy. "Now Mr. Kilpatrick won't have any birthday cake at his party."

Billy looked as though he might cry.

"Never mind now," said his mother. "It was an accident. You didn't mean to smash the cake."

"'Course I didn't," said Billy, "but there won't be any birthday cake for the party and you can't have a birthday party without cake."

Mrs. Porter started the car again. "Well, it can't be helped," she said.

When Betsy and Billy walked into school, their faces did not look cheerful. The children were busy piling their presents for Mr. Kilpatrick on a big tray. There was a sign Ellen had made that said, "Happy Birthday, Mr. Kilpatrick."

When the children saw Billy they called out, "Where's the birthday cake? Did you bring the birthday cake?"

Billy hung his head. "I sat on it," he mumbled.

"What?" cried the children. "What did you say?"

"He sat on it," said Betsy.

"Sat on it!" cried Kenny.

And then the children turned to each other and said, "He sat on it."

"He didn't do it on purpose," said Betsy. "It was an accident."

"Miss Ross," cried Christopher, "now we haven't any birthday cake for Mr. Kilpatrick."

Suddenly, above the voices of the children, the bell sounded for school to begin.

"Take your seats, boys and girls," said Miss Ross. The children went to their seats. There were no happy faces.

"Now cheer up!" said Miss Ross. "There will be plenty of ice cream and all of these lovely presents. Mr. Kilpatrick will be delighted."

"But whoever heard of a birthday party without a cake?" said Kenny.

"I don't want to hear anything more about the cake," said Miss Ross. "Billy is sorry, but you can't put a birthday cake together again."

"Miss Ross, what did Mr. Kilpatrick say when you asked him to come today and see our art exhibit?" said Ellen.

"Oh, he said he would be glad to come," said Miss Ross.

"You don't think he guessed that it was a surprise party, do you?" asked Christopher.

"I don't think he had any idea," said his teacher.

"He would never guess we even know it's his birthday," said Betsy. "I'll bet he doesn't remember he ever told me. On my birthday I told him it was my birthday and I said, 'When is your birthday, Mr. Kilpatrick?' And he said, 'Oh, I blew in on a windy day in March—the thirteenth. It's always been my lucky day.'"

"I guess he'll think it's his lucky day when he sees all those presents," said Ellen.

"All right, now," said Miss Ross, "we have a lot of work to do before the birthday party. Let's begin our spelling lesson."

The morning seemed very long to the children, but at last it was time for lunch. As they stood in line to go to the lunchroom, Miss Ross said, "Now remember, boys and girls! Return to the classroom as soon as you have finished your lunch."

"We won't forget," said Mary Lou, "'cause there's going to be ice cream and cake."

"No cake," the boys shouted.

Billy's face turned bright red.

"Well, there will be ice cream," said Miss Ross.

"And Mr. Kilpatrick," said Betsy. "I hope he doesn't come before we get back."

The children were back in such a short time that Miss Ross, who had stayed in the room, had not finished her own sandwich.

"Has he come?" one child after another asked, looking around the room.

"Not yet," said Miss Ross. "And remember! Not a word about his birthday until Betsy brings in the tray with the presents. The tray is in the coatroom. And then I'll bring in the ice cream."

In a few minutes Mr. Kilpatrick stood in the doorway. The big policeman was smiling broadly. In one hand he was holding his hat and in the other a big box.

"Here he is!" the children shouted. "Here's Mr. Kilpatrick!"

"Come in, Mr. Kilpatrick," said Miss Ross.

"Glad to be here," said Mr. Kilpatrick, walking to Miss Ross's desk. There he deposited his hat and the big box. Every eye in the room was on the box.

"I've got a little surprise for you boys and girls," he said, and he began to open the box. "Today happens to be my birthday and"—here he lifted the lid—"Mrs. Kilpatrick, she knew that I was coming up here at lunchtime and she made me a birthday cake."

Mr. Kilpatrick lifted a great cake out of the box. "I thought I'd like to share it with you boys and girls," he said.

"Oh, boy! That's some cake!" cried Christopher.

It was indeed a handsome cake. It was as fine as the one Billy had sat on, only it had white icing and pink trimmings. The children all crowded around to read what it said on the top. It said "Happy Birthday."

"Mrs. Kilpatrick didn't have any candles," said Mr. Kilpatrick, "but I told her that she couldn't have put them all on, anyway. The cake would have broken down with the weight of 'em."

Billy ran to the coatroom and reached into his coat pocket. When he returned he said, "I've got some candles, Mr. Kilpatrick. I've got twenty-four candles."

"Well, now! What do you know about that!" said Mr. Kilpatrick. "Here, you stick them on."

Billy stepped up to the cake and began poking the candles into the icing.

"Billy sat on his birthday cake," said Kenny.

"He did!" said Mr. Kilpatrick. "Well, I'm mighty glad he didn't sit on mine."

"But he did," several children shouted.

Mr. Kilpatrick looked very puzzled, but just at that moment Betsy came in with the tray piled high with packages. Miss Ross followed with the ice cream. The children began to sing, "Happy birthday to you." Then they shouted, "Happy birthday, Mr. Kilpatrick!"

Mr. Kilpatrick looked very surprised when Betsy handed him the tray full of packages. "Are these all for me?" he asked.

"Yes!" cried the children.

"Well, I . . . I . . . don't know what to say," said Mr. Kilpatrick. "I thought I had a surprise for you and now you have given me a bigger surprise. I guess I can only say thank you. Thank you very much! They look like wonderful presents."

By this time Miss Ross had lit the candles on

the cake. Several of the children were passing the ice cream around.

"Now, Mr. Kilpatrick," said Miss Ross, "you must blow out the candles."

Mr. Kilpatrick gave a mighty blow and out went every candle. Then Miss Ross handed him a knife and he began to cut the cake. The children's mouths were watering by the time they each received a slice. It was delicious cake. Betsy thought it might even be better than Mrs. Porter's.

When the bell rang for the afternoon session, Mr. Kilpatrick stood up to go. "Well, I'm sorry I can't open all of these presents while I'm here," he said, "but I'll open them when I get home. This has been the nicest birthday I ever had." Then, looking around, he said, "I like your art exhibit, too. Very fine indeed."

That evening Mr. Kilpatrick sat at the kitchen table opening his birthday presents. He passed each one to Mrs. Kilpatrick and she said, "My! isn't that a handsome necktie?" and "What could be nicer than those pencils with your name on them?"

When Mr. Kilpatrick opened Betsy's package,

he said, "Now just look at that belt buckle!"

Mrs. Kilpatrick looked at it carefully. "It looks something like your badge," she said.

"Does at that," said Mr. Kilpatrick.

"It's even got some letters on it," said Mrs. Kilpatrick. "Words, I think."

Mr. Kilpatrick took the buckle in his hand again. "I believe it has," he said, "but I can't read it."

"Here, take the magnifying glass," said Mrs. Kilpatrick.

Mr. Kilpatrick held the magnifying glass over the buckle. "Well, what do you know about that!" he said.

"What does it say?" asked his wife.

"It says, 'Member of the Fire Department,'" said Mr. Kilpatrick.

"The Fire Department!" exclaimed Mrs. Kilpatrick. "Well, they're nice lads in the fire department."

"Sure!" said Mr. Kilpatrick. "It's a nice buckle and nobody'll ever be looking at my belt buckle through a magnifying glass."

Eight

Ellen Has a Birthday

Ellen and Betsy were very best friends. They always played together in the school yard. Sometimes Ellen would go home with Betsy after school and sometimes Betsy went with Ellen. Betsy lived in a bigger house than Ellen and Betsy had more toys, but Ellen had a baby sister. Ellen had a Grandmother, too. She lived at Ellen's house. Grandmother knew how to make cinnamon buns and always remembered that children liked cinnamon buns to be very sticky. So Betsy loved to visit Ellen just as much as Ellen liked to visit Betsy. Sometimes Ellen stayed overnight at Betsy's house and slept in the bed beside Betsy's. The girls found this great fun. Betsy loved it because it made her feel as though she had a sister. Betsy was looking forward to the day when she would have a real sister. It wouldn't be long now, because Betsy's mother had told her that there would be a baby around the first of the year. Betsy hoped that it would be a baby sister.

One day Betsy and Ellen met at the Good Lady's store. Betsy was buying a red pencil and Ellen was buying a blue one. The Good Lady kept a tiny store right near the school. She sold ice cream and candy, pencils and notebooks, erasers, crayons and toys. Her name was Mrs. Good but she was called the Good Lady by all the children because she always made the ice cream cones stand up like mountains. No child ever bought a pencil or a notebook from her without receiving a peppermint drop or a jelly bean.

The two girls left the shop together. They were

each sucking a peppermint drop. Outside, they stopped to look in the window. The Good Lady's window was always shiny and clean. "Oh, Betsy," cried Ellen, "look at the little set of doll's dishes." Right in the center of the window there was a box filled with the prettiest dishes Betsy had ever seen. There were six tiny cups, no bigger than thimbles, and six tiny saucers. There was a little teapot, a sugar bowl, and a cream pitcher. Each piece had a bright pink rose painted on it. All were carefully packed in pink cotton. "I would love to have those dishes for my birthday," said Ellen.

Ellen's birthday was only two weeks off. Ellen had been talking about her birthday for a long time. It was a very important birthday because Ellen would be seven years old. She wished that she could have a party, but Ellen's father worked at night and he had to sleep in the daytime, so the children could never have parties. Ellen would not be able to have a party. But there would be presents. Ellen said there were always presents even if you didn't have a party.

After school, Betsy stopped at the window again to look at the dishes. How she would love to give those pretty little dishes to Ellen for her birthday! Betsy decided that she would take all of the money out of her bank. She would buy the dishes with the money. Betsy's little bank was a round, fat, yellow duck. He opened his wide bill and swallowed pennies. Betsy called him Big Bill. She wondered whether Big Bill had swallowed enough pennies to pay for the dishes. Father gave Betsy some brand-new pennies every week. She had been putting half of them in Big Bill. "But now I will put all of them in," thought Betsy. She fed every one of Father's pennies to Big Bill. When Mother gave her money for candy, Betsy dropped it in her bank. Big Bill grew heavier and heavier. When Betsy shook him he rattled loudly and made Betsy feel very rich. She was sure that she would be able to buy the dishes very soon.

Every day Betsy stopped at the store window to look at the pretty dishes. Two days before Ellen's birthday, her mother drove Betsy to school. When Betsy and her mother reached the school, Betsy said, "Mother, please come look at the little dishes in the Good Lady's window." Mother was in a hurry, but she stepped out of the car and went with Betsy to look in the shop window. "Aren't they lovely little dishes, Mother?" asked Betsy. "I want to buy them—"

"Not now," interrupted her mother. "We can talk about them when there is more time. Run along now, Betsy."

Betsy ran along to school and her mother drove away.

That afternoon when school was over, Betsy stopped again to look in the window. The dishes were gone. Betsy couldn't believe her eyes. The dishes had been there that morning and now there was just an empty space where they had been. Betsy had never thought that someone else might buy them. She had thought of them always as Ellen's dishes. "Perhaps," thought Betsy, "the Good Lady still has them inside." She opened the door of the shop. The sleigh bells hanging on the door jingled. Betsy walked up to the counter. The Good Lady smiled and said, "Well, my dear?"

"Where are the little dishes?" asked Betsy, pointing to the window.

"I just sold them an hour ago," said the Good Lady. "Were you thinking of buying them?" she asked. Betsy nodded her head. "Now that's too bad," said the Good Lady. "Perhaps I have something else you would like?" But Betsy did not like anything else. She had set her heart on the dishes for Ellen and now they were gone. Betsy walked home feeling very sad.

When she reached home, Mother was sitting in the library. She was sewing. When she saw Betsy's sad little face, she said, "Why, what's happened to Mother's little sunshine?"

Betsy ran to her mother. "Oh, Mother," she cried, "the dishes are gone. Now I can't give them to Ellen for her birthday."

Mother lifted her little girl on her lap. "Betsy, darling," she said, "I didn't know that you wanted to give the dishes to Ellen." Betsy hid her face on Mother's shoulder. "Look at Koala over there in the corner," said Mother.

Betsy looked and there sat her toy koala bear, having a tea party all by himself. There were six little cups and saucers, the teapot, the sugar bowl, and cream pitcher all spread out in front of him. Betsy couldn't believe her eyes. "Where did they come from, Mother?" she asked.

"I bought them on my way home," replied Mother. "I thought my little girl wanted them."

"Oh, no," said Betsy, "I wanted to buy them for Ellen with my own money. Big Bill is full of pennies that I saved."

"Ellen can still have her present," said Mother. "I have saved the box."

"And the pink cotton?" asked Betsy

"Yes, and the pink cotton," replied her mother.

"Oh, thank you," said Betsy. "It's a lovely present, isn't it, Mother?"

Betsy's mother had invited Ellen and her mother and Ellen's baby sister to spend the Saturday afternoon of Ellen's birthday. When they arrived Betsy ran to the door to meet them. Betsy was wearing a beautiful long dress with a ruffle on the bottom. It was a white dress with tiny blue forget-me-nots all over it. Blue party shoes peeked out from under Betsy's dress.

Ellen's mouth opened when she saw Betsy.

"Oh, Betsy!" she cried. "You look beautiful! Are you going to a party?"

"Yes, I am," Betsy replied.

Ellen looked down at her own clothes, at her blue jeans and her tan sweater. "I wish I were going to a party," she said, "but I couldn't go to a party. I look like Cinderella."

Betsy laughed. "But you are going to a party, Ellen," she said.

"Oh, no," said Ellen, "not in these clothes. Like I said, I'm just Cinderella."

Ellen's mother jumped up and placed the baby on the sofa. "No, you're not Cinderella! Just wait until I unpack this box that has been waiting here at Betsy's."

Ellen's eyes grew very big as she watched her mother unpack the box and remove large pieces of tissue paper. Then she saw her mother take a dress from the box and when her mother held it up it was exactly like Betsy's, but the flowers were pink instead of blue.

Ellen clapped her hands and cried, "Oh, it's beautiful!"

"That isn't all," said Betsy, "just see what my mother has for you."

Then Betsy's mother handed a box to Ellen and said, "Happy birthday!"

"Oh, thank you," said Ellen, who was already pulling her sweater over her head.

When Ellen opened the box she found a pair of pink party shoes. "Oh!" she cried. "I can't wait to put everything on."

Ellen didn't wait. In a few minutes she was no longer Cinderella but she looked ready for a ball.

"Now you are ready for the party," Betsy cried, "and you look beautiful."

"But where is the party?" Ellen asked.

Betsy laughed. "Why, it's right here. It's your party, Ellen," she said.

Ellen was so surprised she couldn't think of anything to say except, "Really! Oh, my!"

Then Betsy handed Ellen the little box and said, "Happy birthday, Ellen."

Ellen unwrapped the paper from around the box. Betsy held her breath as Ellen lifted the lid. Slowly, Ellen lifted one end of the pink cotton and looked underneath. When she saw the pink and white tea set she said, "Oh, my little dishes." Then Betsy and Ellen began to laugh because they were so happy. They danced around the room twirling their ruffled skirts.

After a while Billy Porter arrived. He had a package for Ellen. When she opened it she found six pretty handkerchiefs. In a few minutes Kenny Roberts came. He had a present for Ellen, too. Then came Mary Lou and Betty Jane and Peter and Christopher. They each had a present for Ellen. Ellen was so surprised and so happy she didn't know what to do, but she did remember to say "Thank you."

After the children had played some games, Betsy's mother took them into the playroom. There were a table and eight chairs. In the center of the table there was a birthday cake. It was covered with white frosting and decorated with pink roses. It had seven lighted pink candles. Ellen thought it was the most beautiful birthday cake she had ever seen. The children sat down and Betsy's mother brought them plates of pink ice cream. Then Ellen, with one puff, blew out the candles. Everyone laughed and clapped hands. Betsy's mother cut each of the children a slice of birthday cake.

Ellen picked a candy rose off of her cake and said, "This rose looks like the roses on my tea set." Ellen took the tea set out of the box and the children around the table admired the little dishes. Ellen placed the candy rose on a plate and laughed when she saw it filled the plate. Then she noticed Betsy's koala sitting on the floor in the corner of the room. "Oh!" she said. "Koala should have some birthday cake." She jumped up and carried the tea set to the koala. She placed all of the dishes in front of the toy bear, with a tiny piece of birthday cake on some of the plates. "Now," she said, "the koala bear is sharing my birthday party."

Ellen had just returned to her place at the table when Thumpy, Betsy's cocker spaniel, came rushing into the room. Thumpy ran right to Koala and dishes flew around the floor in front of Koala. Thumpy lost no time licking up the pieces of cake and the sugar rose. "Oh!" cried Ellen. "My dishes."

"Thumpy!" Betsy called out. "Oh, Thumpy! Look what you did!"

Thumpy was licking his chops and begging at Billy's chair for more cake. Ellen got down on her knees to pick up her dishes. "Oh, no!" she exclaimed. "I can't find the lid to the teapot. Oh, no."

Now all of the children had left the table and were trying to help Ellen find the lid to the teapot. "We'll just have a new game," said Betsy's mother. "This game is called Hunt the Lid."

"Will there be a prize?" said Billy Porter.

"Of course," said Betsy. "There's always a prize for a game."

Now all of the children were on their hands and knees looking for the lid of the teapot. "It's so tiny," said Ellen. "Oh, I do hope we find it."

"Sure we'll find it!" said Billy. "It didn't fly out the window."

The children spent the next half-hour crawling around the floor. They looked behind table legs, under chairs, in every corner, but the little lid stayed hidden. Billy kept singing, "Come, little liddy, come, little liddy!"

Suddenly Billy cried out, "I've got it! I've got it!" Billy held up the tiny lid.

"Where was it?" Ellen said.

"It was right here on the chair," said Billy. "It did fly, when Thumpy pounced on those dishes."

"But not out the window," said Ellen, "and I'm glad you found it, Billy."

Billy put the lid back on the teapot. "Do I get the prize?" he said.

"Of course you get the prize," said Betsy's mother. "And here it is."

Billy held out his hand to receive a new blue pencil. "Thanks," he said.

"Oh!" cried Betsy. "That looks like the blue pencil I bought at the Good Lady's."

"It is," said her mother. "But you can use some of that money you have in Big Bill to buy another blue pencil. Don't be stingy!"

Betsy and all her friends laughed.

That night, when Ellen's father went into her

room for a good-night kiss, Ellen was very sleepy. When her father leaned over her bed, he heard her say, "I had a birthday party. Pink candles and dishes. I'm not Cinderella, Daddy."

"No," indeed," said her father, although he didn't know what Ellen was talking about, he was glad Ellen had had such a good time.

Nine

Betsy's Birthday Wish

Betsy was spending the summer on her grandfather's farm. She had spent every summer on the farm with her grandfather and grandmother since she was a very little girl, and she had grown to love the farm. The farm was made up of cornfields and tomato crops. Grandmother had enough chickens to keep her refrigerator stocked with eggs and to supply the country store. Betsy had helped her grandmother gather eggs every

morning since Betsy had been four years old.
Now she was eight and there were many things
she could do to help around the farm. She was
sitting with her grandmother on the porch helping her shell lima beans when a boy from a
nearby farm came up the road on a bicycle, rais-
ing a cloud of dust. He waved to Betsy and she
called out, "Hi, Danny!" Then she turned to her
grandmother and said, "It's too bad there isn't
any sidewalk or even any paving in the road.
There's no place to roller-skate."

"You don't have any roller skates here with
you," said her grandmother.

"No," said Betsy. "I don't have any roller
skates at all. My friend Ellen has roller skates and
so does Billy Porter. I think it would be wonderful
to have roller skates. I see skaters on TV, and
they even dance on roller skates."

"Dance!" exclaimed her grandmother. "I hope
you'll never try to dance on roller skates. You'll
go slithering all over the place!"

Betsy laughed. "Don't worry, Granny," she
said. "I don't have the roller skates. But I hope to

get them for Christmas. Or maybe for my birthday, next April."

"I don't know why you're so set on having roller skates," said her grandmother. "Here you've got old Rosie the horse to ride, and you ride in the pickup truck when you go to town with Gramp every time he takes corn and tomatoes to the market. Ain't that wheels enough?"

"Of course I love Rosie," said Betsy. "But Rosie doesn't have wheels!" Now Betsy and her grandmother laughed until tears came, as they thought of Rosie on roller skates.

The following morning Betsy went with her grandfather when he took his load of corn and tomatoes into the town market. Betsy loved to go with her grandfather, for she knew that after he had delivered his corn and tomatoes she and Gramp would walk around the town and look in the shop windows and stop in the town diner for a snack. It was usually a hamburger or a hot dog.

Today they were eating hamburgers when a boy came in wearing roller skates. He left with a hot dog. When the boy left, Betsy said to her grandfather, "Oh, Gramp! Did you see those roller skates that boy was wearing? They were very special. They had boots with them. I guess he lives here in town, where there are plenty of cement walks. Of course, when I'm home there are lots of places to roller-skate. Only I haven't any skates. I do wish I had roller skates!"

"Roller skates!" exclaimed her grandfather. "You'd just be skinning your knees, bloodying your nose, maybe break your arm."

Betsy giggled. "Oh, Gramp. I wouldn't do any of those things. My friends don't fall and break things. I would be a good skater. I could even learn to dance."

"Dance on roller skates!" exclaimed her grandfather. "Balderdash!"

"Balderdash!" Betsy repeated. "That's a funny word."

"It's what I say when I don't like something," said her grandfather. "Balderdash to dancing on skates."

"Balderdash sounds like something to eat," said Betsy. "Won't you try some balderdash? It's very much like pepper hash. Or maybe you like succotash. Oh, do try a bit of balderdash."

Betsy's grandfather laughed. "You're just trying to take my mind off roller skates," he said.

"Oh, no, Gramp," said Betsy. "I'm just trying to take your mind off bloody noses and broken arms. I want you to think about the skates and how much I want them."

"You're just trying to soften me up," said her grandfather.

"Oh, I wouldn't do that," said Betsy. "That would be hinting. And Mother says that is very rude."

"Well, I got the message," said her grandfather. "But I don't intend to help you get skinned knees and a bloody nose."

Betsy laughed. "I'm glad you gave up the broken arm."

"That's right," said her grandfather. "Well, maybe you wouldn't get a broken arm."

"Great," said Betsy. "I'm glad you've given me back my arm!"

When Betsy and her grandfather left the diner,

they walked around the shopping mall and looked in the shop windows. Soon they came to a sporting goods store. In the center of the window, beside some ski boots, was a pair of boots with roller skates.

"Oh, Gramp!" cried Betsy. "Look at those beautiful roller skates with boots! They're just like the ones that boy in the diner was wearing."

"I see them," said her grandfather. "And I see you with skinned knees!"

"I'm glad now I don't have a bloody nose," said Betsy.

Her grandfather laughed. "I am not buying skates," he said.

Betsy took hold of her grandfather's arm and looked up into his face. "Couldn't we just go in and try them on?" she coaxed.

"All right," said her grandfather. "You can try them on."

Inside the store they sat down. A salesman came and said, "What can I do for you, sir?"

"Those roller skates in the window," said Grandfather.

"Certainly," said the salesman. "For yourself, sir?"

Betsy giggled.

"I should say not!" said her grandfather. "Roller skates are not for me!"

"Oh," said the salesman. "Many senior citizens are roller-skating today. Very fine exercise."

"Balderdash!" Grandfather exploded.

Betsy giggled again. And under her breath her grandfather heard her say, "Won't you try some balderdash?"

Now her grandfather chuckled. "It's my granddaughter here who wants to see the skates."

"Very good, sir," said the salesman, as he sat down to measure Betsy's foot. "Aha," he said. "A four-and-a-half boot will fit nicely."

The salesman went off, but when he came back, he said, "I'm sorry, but I'm out of the young lady's size. We will be getting them in, of course. I can always send them to you, if you'll just leave your name and address."

To Betsy's disappointment, her grandfather did not leave any name and address. For a few minutes Betsy had thought she was very close to her roller skates, but they seemed to have rolled away.

As Betsy and her grandfather climbed back into the truck, her grandfather, seeing the disappointment on Betsy's face, said, "You couldn't have skated on the farm anyway."

"I know," said Betsy, swallowing a sob.

The summer days flew by, and soon Grandfather was gathering the last of his corn. Grandmother's kitchen was filled with the smell of tomato preserves and catsup. All too soon the day arrived when Betsy took her last ride on Rosie, and in the afternoon Betsy's father came to take her home. The time had come for Betsy to say good-bye to her grandparents.

As Christmas drew near, Betsy's heart quickened with the arrival of each parcel, always hoping that it would contain the roller skates. But Christmas came and went, and there were no roller skates for Betsy.

"I guess Gramp really doesn't want me to have roller skates," said Betsy to her mother. "But maybe he'll change his mind and send them to me for my birthday."

Now Betsy began looking forward to her birthday in April. The snow would be gone, and roller skates and jumping ropes would be out under the budding trees. When Betsy's friends called out, "Oh, Betsy, it's such fun to roller-skate," Betsy would call back, "Maybe I'll get them for my birthday. I hope so."

As Betsy's birthday drew near, she watched every day for parcels. When she came in from school, she would ask her mother, "Anything come for me today?"

One day there was a small parcel for Betsy, but she knew at once that it did not contain roller skates. A few days later there was another parcel, and although Betsy could tell it did not contain roller skates, she felt excited when she saw it, for it had come all the way from Scotland. It was from her Auntie Ruth, who was visiting friends.

Betsy kept right on hoping that the roller skates would arrive, for there were still three days before her birthday, and no parcel from her grandfather had yet come. There were moments when she wondered whether Gramp didn't like her hinting about buying roller skates.

When Betsy's birthday arrived, nothing had come from her grandfather. Her mother gave her a book written by Betsy's favorite author, and her father gave her a new game that looked like fun. When she opened the little parcel that had come in the mail, Betsy found a gold bracelet, with small gold letters dangling from it. The letters spelled "Betsy." It was from her grandmother, with a loving message. Betsy thought it was beautiful.

Inside the parcel from Scotland Betsy found a bright red sweater and a tartan skirt. She was delighted and thought of herself out roller skating in her red sweater and tartan skirt.

But in spite of all these lovely presents, and in spite of a beautiful birthday cake and chocolate ice cream after dinner, Betsy felt sad, because Gramp had forgotten her birthday.

Just as Betsy had finished her cake and ice cream, there was a ring at the front door. Betsy jumped down from her chair. "Maybe it's the delivery man!" she cried. Betsy rushed ahead of her father and opened the front door.

It was indeed a delivery man, with a parcel that looked like a shoe box.

"Oh, Daddy!" cried Betsy, as her father took the parcel from the man. "I bet it's roller skates from Gramp! Quick, open it!"

Betsy's father carried the parcel to the kitchen. Betsy watched as he opened the box and lifted out a pair of boots with roller skates. With a beaming face, Betsy read the card that said, "Happy Birthday and Happy Landings!"

Then she sat down and put on the boots. But when she stood up there was a clatter, and her feet went from under her. She sat down with a thud.

Her father helped her up. Betsy laughed. "I guess I won't be dancing very soon," she said.

When Billy Porter learned that Betsy's wish for roller skates had finally come true, he said, "I'll teach you how to skate, Betsy! I'll come over after school tomorrow."

"Oh, thanks, Billy," said Betsy. "I can hardly wait to go skating!"

The following day, when Billy arrived at Betsy's house, Billy was wearing his skates. Betsy admired the ease with which Billy rolled around. It looked so simple. Betsy was certain that in a few minutes she would be doing the same thing. But when she stood up, her wheels went from under her, and just as she had the day before, she went down kerplunk. She rubbed herself and said, "Oh, my poor beedy dum!"

"Your what?" said Billy.

"My beedy dum," said Betsy. "That's what I've always called that part of myself."

"Well, I call it my bottom," said Billy.

"Now show me what to do," said Betsy.

"It's easy," said Billy, taking hold of Betsy's hand. "But you can't skate with stiff legs. You have to bend your knees."

Betsy tried to bend her knees. But again her skates went from under her and once more with a clatter she sat down hard. Both Betsy and Billy laughed. "It's not as easy as you thought, is it,

Betsy?" said Billy. "But you'll catch on. Tomorrow's Saturday, and I'll come over."

"Oh, thanks," said Betsy, still rubbing herself.

The following morning Betsy came upon her cocker spaniel, Thumpy, as he was beating up an old sofa pillow, growling all the while. Thumpy beat it up several times a day. It was his favorite toy. "Oh, Thumpy!" Betsy cried. "That's just what I need. Let me borrow your cushion."

Thumpy was not anxious to lend his cushion to Betsy. When she took hold of it, Thumpy put up a fight, shaking the pillow and growling. But in the end Betsy won. Then with her skipping rope, she tied the pillow on the place she called her beedy dum.

When Billy arrived, he looked at Betsy and cried out, "Are you crazy? What's all that pillow for, and all that rope?"

"It's for protection," said Betsy. "It hurts when I bump myself."

"Well, never mind your whatchamacallit," said Billy. "You'll never be able to skate with your legs tied with that rope! Come on. Everybody can learn to skate, so you can learn to skate. Take off that pillow and let's get going."

Betsy untied the rope and threw Thumpy's cushion on the step at the front door. Then she put on her skates. Billy took hold of Betsy's hand. "Now," he said, "bend your knees and roll! Bend—roll."

In a few minutes Betsy was skating by herself. "Hurray!" cried Billy. "You've got it!"

Betsy laughed. She was delighted to be roller skating at last.

When Betsy wrote a thank-you note for the skates to her grandfather, she added, "No skinned knees! No bloody nose! Nothing broken! Love from Betsy."

ABOUT THE AUTHOR

CAROLYN HAYWOOD was born in Philadelphia and now lives in Chestnut Hill, a suburb of that city. A graduate of the Philadelphia Normal School, she also studied at the Pennsylvania Academy of Fine Arts, where she won the Cresson European Scholarship. Her first story, *"B" Is for Betsy*, was published in 1939. Since then she has written books almost every year and has become one of the most widely read American writers for younger children.

ABOUT THE ILLUSTRATOR

WENDY WATSON hails from a family of writers and artists. She herself is both a successful illustrator and author of books for children. Her books have been chosen best of the year by *The New York Times* and *School Library Journal* and selected by the Junior Literary Guild. Wendy Watson lives with her two children in East Corinth, Vermont.